I WAS A (

THE AUTOBIOGRAPHY OF

ERNST TOLLER

Contents

1. Childhood

My maternal great-grandfather received permission from Frederick the Great to settle as the only Jew in Samotschin, a little town in the Netzebruch near the Polish border. My great-grandfather paid for this privilege with money. It was a thing of which his great-grandson was very proud; I used to brag about it to my school-fellows, and dreamed of advancement and ennoblement.

My paternal great-grandfather, who was of Spanish extraction, had an estate in West Prussia, and an aunt of mine used to relate that he ate off golden dishes while his horse fed from a silver manger; but with his sons the manger had become copper and the dishes mere silver. As a boy I used to dream of these legendary riches: in my dreams the old man was devoured by his horse, while I looked on placidly and unsympathetically; indeed, rather with an unaccountable feeling of satisfaction.

In my grandparents' house the loft was full of huge, dusty old folios, heavily gilt. My grandfather used to read them all day and sometimes even all night, while my grandmother ran the shop, served the customers, and did the housekeeping. This was the business that my father inherited after a brilliant career at the University and some time as a chemist.

Samotschin was an intensely German town, and both Protestants and Jews were proud of the fact. They spoke with scorn of the other towns in Posen, where no distinction was made between Catholics and Poles. Ostmark had first come into Prussia's hands with the second Partition; but the Germans regarded themselves as hereditary rulers, merely tolerating the Poles. These little villages of the plain, invaded by German colonists, acted as outposts, as buffer territory between Germany proper and the Polish estates and farmland. Poles and Germans fought relentlessly over every foot of land; and any German who sold land to a Pole was regarded as a traitor.

We children called the Poles "Polacks" and firmly believed that they were the descendants of Cain, who slew Abel and was branded by God.

Against the Poles, Jews and Germans showed a united front. The Jews looked upon themselves as the pioneers of German culture, and their houses in these little towns became cultural centers where German literature, philosophy and art were cultivated with a pride and an assiduousness which bordered on the ridiculous. The Poles were declared to be no patriots—the poor Poles whose children at school were forbidden their mother-tongue, whose lands had been confiscated by the German State. But on the Kaiser's birthday the Jews sat at the same table as the Reserve officers, the War League, and the Home Defense Corps, and drank beer and schnapps and raised their glasses to the Kaiser's health.

I was born on the first of December, 1893. Looking back on my childhood days I find myself remembering disconnected and fragmentary incidents.

I see myself wearing a little short dress, standing outside our house looking at a cart. It is big, bigger than Marie, as big as a house. Marie is the nurse, and she wears a red coral necklace—round, red corals. She is sitting on one of the shafts, rocking to and fro. Then Ilse comes out with her nurse. She runs up to me and we hold hands; for some time we stand hand in hand and look at each other curiously. Ilse's nurse is gossiping with Marie, but suddenly she calls out:

"Come away, Ilse! He's a Jew."

Ilse drops my hand and runs away. I can't understand what the nurse means, but I begin to cry bitterly. At last the other nurse departs with Ilse, and Marie tries to comfort me, taking me in her arms and showing me her corals; but I don't want the corals, and I break her necklace.

I am friends with the night-watchman's son. When the others cry "Polack" I cry "Polack" with them; but he is my friend for all that. His name is Stanislaus, and he tells me how the Polacks hate the Germans.

In the market-place they have been taking up the pavement and digging trenches. It is Saturday night, and the workmen have left their spades and pick-axes in a little hut made of rough boards while they go to the public house. Stanislaus and I sit in one of the trenches, a narrow ditch covered with planks. Stanislaus spits.

"Tonight one of the workmen will die as a punishment for digging here. They've no right to dig here; it's Polish earth. The Germans stole it from us. But let 'em go on digging just here where they've begun, let 'em go on digging another hundred yards down, and they'll come upon the King of Poland. He has a white horse in his stable, so beautiful that the Captain's horse would look like a billy-goat beside it. When the time comes, the King of Poland will mount his horse and ride up from below the earth and drive them all away. All of them. You as well."

I ask Stanislaus when that time will come. Stanislaus knows more than I do, for his father is the night-watchman. But he presses his lips together and sets his mouth obstinately.

"Spit then, and give me a marble as pledge."

I spit and he takes the marble but says nothing. All night I dream that Stanislaus is standing in the market-place blowing on his father's horn. And suddenly a white horse comes galloping out of our ditch, its brown saddle covered with Kaiser-pictures.

I collect Kaiser-pictures. In my father's shop there are lots of fascinating things, string, bonbons, lemonade and raisins, little nails and big nails; but best of all are the Kaiser-pictures. And they are the hardest to steal. There is one in every packet of chocolate; but the chocolate cupboard is kept locked, and the key is on a bunch which Mother carries in her blue checked apron. Mother is always working; she is working when I wake up in the morning. She works in the shop, in the granary, she does the housekeeping, she gives food to the poor and invites beggars in to the midday meal, and when the farmhand goes to the fields to plow and sow it is to her he comes for supplies. Every evening she sits reading, deep into the night, often falling asleep over her book. And if I wake her up she says:

"Do let me be, child, reading is the only pleasure I have."

"Why are you always working, Mother?"

"Because you must eat, my dear."

If Mother isn't careful I steal the key, and then the pictures out of the packets of chocolate. The chocolate itself is only incidental. They are beautiful pictures of ancient Germans, dressed in skins and leaning on huge clubs; their women squat beside them polishing their shields. Stanislaus thinks they used their blond hair to polish the shields with, hair which looks like straw bed-hangings. In most of the packets there are pictures of our own Kaiser wearing a red velvet cloak over his shoulders and holding a ball in one hand and a gold poker in the other.

I am lying in bed one morning, looking at my Kaiser-pictures, and I ask myself if the Kaiser ever has to go to the bathroom like me. The question worries me, and I run to Mother.

"You will finish up in prison," says Mother.

So the Kaiser does *not* go to the bathroom.

The street between the church and the market-place is called the Totenstrasse, the Street of the Dead; but the people who live there don't see any particular sense in the name. They stand at their doors and gossip, grumbling at the burgomaster because the pavement (of which everybody in the town is very proud) stops halfway up the street. "As if it had been cut off with a knife," says Herr Fischer the dealer. I am glad I don't live in the Totenstrasse. I have never seen a dead man, only once a skull and some bones that the workmen dug up when they were making a well near the mill. Stanislaus and I played ball with the skull, using the bones as bats; and Stanislaus gave the skull a kick.

"Why did you kick it?"

"Grandmother said he was a wicked men. Good people don't stay in their graves. Angels come and fly away with them to Heaven."

"What do they do there?"

"Well, they don't eat potatoes in their skins."

I like potatoes baked in their skins, not at home

but with Stanislaus. His grandmother, his mother and father, his three sisters and four brothers all live in the Dorfstrasse in a little house made of mud with a thatched roof. They all sleep in one room, which gets very hot. There is no pavement in the Dorfstrasse, but nobody thinks of complaining to the burgomaster about it. When I go and see Stanislaus at dinner-time I find them all eating baked potatoes and groats or baked potatoes and pickled herring. I stand in a corner watching them with my mouth watering.

At last Stanislaus' mother tells me to help myself. "If there's enough for eleven, one more won't make much difference."

Stanislaus digs me in the ribs.

"You can imagine it's roast meat."

"We don't have roast meat every day."

"You could if you wanted to."

I take up my cap and run home.

"You oughtn't to go there for dinner," Mother says to me, "eating their food when they have so little."

"Why haven't they got more?"

"Because it's God's will."

The Totenstrasse is very long—I suppose to give the dead on their way to the churchyard a chance to decide whether they would rather stay in their graves or fly up to Heaven.

Uncle M. has just died. I wonder very much if he was a good man. I go to the churchyard, break off a branch of yew, whittle it, and sharpen the end. Then I climb the wall and bore down into uncle's grave to see if he is still there. But the sexton surprises me, and I run away.

On the way home I ask myself, What is a good man?

I hear doors slamming outside. It ought to be dark in the room. Father sleeps there, and Mother over there. But it isn't dark now, and their beds are empty. Have they been kidnaped? There is a red glare outside. Somebody is blowing a horn, on and on, a wailing note. I jump out of bed, wrench open the door and run out into the street; and there on the other side of the market-place is a house on fire, all red and green and black. Firemen with shining helmets are running about wildly, and a gaping crowd stands watching it all. Julie, our cook, catches sight of me and drives me back to bed.

"Why is that house on fire, Julie?"

"Because God always punishes people."

"But why does He want to?"

"Because little children ask too many questions."

I am frightened, and I can't get to sleep again—the night smells of smoke and of burning; it smells of God.

In the morning I stand looking at the charred wood and blackened stone, still hot.

"They haven't found so much as a button; the poor thing must have been burned to ashes in her bed."

I turn round quickly, but the man who was speaking has gone on.

I run home and sit down in a corner, still clasping the stick I was poking the ashes with.

Herr Levi comes and laughs at me.

"A nice thing you've done."

I don't move.

"The whole town knows it was you who set fire to Eichstädt's house."

Herr Levi lights a cigar and goes away. First Julie said I was to blame, and now Herr Levi.

I crawl under the table and stay there till evening. What did I do wrong yesterday? I undressed, I washed myself, went to bed and fell asleep; but I didn't really wash, only promised Mother I would, which was a lie. Is that what caused the fire? Is that the reason for this terrible punishment? Is God so strict? I think of baked potatoes and of Frau Eichstädt burned to death.

It is dark in the room, and I lie there listening. On the right of the door there is a thin circular glass tube, which I am forbidden to touch. Marie, the maid, crosses herself before she dusts it.

"That's where your Jewish God lives," she grumbles; and my heart thumps. I daren't touch it. What if He were to jump out of the tube and cry: "I am the Lord God! I have come to punish you for lying. . . ."

But I won't let myself be frightened any longer by the Lord God in the tube, nor by the thought of baked potatoes; with one leap I am at the door, and climbing onto the chest of drawers I tear the Lord God down. I break the glass tube into bits. He does not appear. I throw it onto the floor. Still He does not appear. I spit on it and stamp on it. The Lord God does nothing. Perhaps He is dead. He surely must be. I gather up the broken glass and paper and stick them down the crack of the sofa: to-morrow I will bury the Lord God.

Back in bed again I feel very happy. Everybody shall hear how I have killed the Lord God dead.

I had always thought that boys and girls all went to the same school. But Paul and Ilse go to the Evangelical school, I go to the Jewish school, and Stanislaus to the Catholic school. But they all learn to read and write just like me, and the school rooms all look just the same. Our teacher is called Herr Senger. When he comes in to take the class we all cry: "Good morning, Herr Senger." He sits down at his desk and puts his pointer in front of him. If you have not done your home work you must hold out your hand, and Herr Senger canes you with his pointer. "That's to punish you." If you have done your home work well Herr Senger takes you on his knee and rubs his prickly cheek against yours. "As a reward," he says.

In recess we compare our sandwiches.

"I've got meat."

"I've got cheese."

"What have you got in yours?"

"He hasn't got anything in his."

Kurt tries to hide his poor sandwich, but we won't let him. We laugh at him, and Kurt cries: "I'll tell my mother on you," and we call back: "Sneak!" Then Kurt throws down his bread and begins crying.

Going home from school, Max says: "My people won't let me play with Kurt; his mother does our washing. Poor people are dirty and have fleas."

I am playing with Stanislaus. I have had a train as a present and now I am the engine-driver and Stanislaus is the signalman. In the middle of the journey I whistle.

"Right away," cries Stanislaus, and whistles shrilly with two fingers in his month.

"Have you got fleas?"

"Right away!"

"Are you dirty?"

Stanislaus kicks the train over, reducing my lovely present to twisted metal.

"Max said all poor people are dirty and have fleas. And now you've broken my train. Do you call yourself my friend?"

"I'm not your friend. I hate you."

In the streets the children cry: "Yah to you, dirty Jew!" I have never heard this before. Stanislaus is the only one who doesn't, and I ask him what it means.

"In Konitz the Jews killed a Christian baby and made Passion-cakes with its blood."

"That's not true."

"Well, is it true that we are dirty and have fleas?"

Herr Senger, the teacher, is crossing the market-place when a boy runs after him and sings:

> "*Jiddchen, Jiddchen, schillemachei,*
> *Reisst dem Juden sein Rock entzwei,*
> *Der Rock ist zerrisen,*
> *Der Jud hat geschissen.*"

Herr Senger goes on without turning his head, and the boy calls out: "Konitz, yah, yah! Konitz, yah, yah!"

"Do you really believe that the Jews killed a Christian baby in Konitz?" I ask Stanislaus. "I'll never eat Passion-cake again."

"Idiot! You can give it to me then."

"Why do they shout, 'Yah, yah, dirty Jew'?"

"Don't you shout 'Polack' after us?"

"That's different."

"Different, hell! If you want to know, Grandmother says it was the Jews killed our Savior on the cross."

I run into the barn and crawl into the straw, feeling miserable. I know the Savior. He hangs in Stanislaus' room; red tears run down his cheeks, and he carries his heart open in his breast and it is all bleeding. Underneath it says: "Suffer little children to come unto me." When I am there and nobody can see me I pray to the Savior.

"Please, dear Savior, forgive me for letting the Jews kill you dead."

When I am in bed I ask Mother: "Why are we Jews?"

"Go to sleep, you naughty boy, and don't ask silly questions."

But I can't go to sleep. I don't want to be a Jew. I don't want the other children to run after me shouting "Dirty Jew!"

In the carpenter's yard there is a hut where the "True Christians" meet. They blow trombones and sing Hallelujah and kneel on the ground and shout, "Thy Kingdom is at hand, O Zion!" Then they embrace one another, and blow their trombones again. I want to be a "True Christian" too, so I follow the others into the hut. The preacher pats me on the head and gives me a lump of sugar and says that I am on the "right path."

"We will all celebrate Christmas together in love and good-will," he says, and I say "Yes."

"And you, my boy, shall have this little Christmas verse to recite."

I am blissfully happy. I am not a Jew any more, and I have a Christmas verse to learn; nobody will ever be able to call "Dirty Jew!" after me again. I take up a trumpet and blow it when the preacher blows his trombone; and then in a clear, solemn voice I recite my Christmas verse. But next day the preacher

23

says he is very sorry, but the Savior would rather Franz recited the verse.

All grown-ups are bad, but if you are cunning you can outwit them. Our gang is very cunning. I am the captain; the other brigands carry short wooden swords, but I have a long one. Old Hordig made it for me. "You look like a real officer," he said, as he hid the cigars I had stolen for him.

We break into the cupboard where Mother keeps the preserved fruits and sample every jar; when the fruit is too sour we pour vinegar into it. In the evenings we slink round the houses and pull the doorbells and run away and laugh at the owners, who are first bewildered and then angry. We stretch string across the street, and jeer when somebody trips over it and falls. We steal money and smoke cigarettes which we pretend to enjoy. We have declared war on all grown-ups. We forget our own quarrels and take a terrible Indian oath that we will wage war to the death on all grown-ups.

Father has given me a little dog, hardly two months old, white with brown spots, a tiny soft bundle of fur that I can hug to my breast, and roll about, and throw up into the air. I am Herr Senger, and I call the dog Puck. I order him to lie down, to be good, to shake hands, to obey. But he won't obey, so I duck him in a tub of cold water. "That's to punish you," I say.

In the morning the puppy is dead. I invite all my friends to the funeral. We dig a grave and solemnly carry the coffin to the graveside. I am the parson. Imitating Herr Senger's voice I say: "This puppy need not have died, but he was disobedient, and now he is punished." A little later my father calls me to his room.

"Here is a letter from the police, saying that you tortured your puppy to death and will have to go to the lock-up. The lock-up is a little hut in the burgomaster's yard where they put tramps. It has no windows, only a door with two locks and two bolts. Herr Mathey, the policeman, pushes them in, slams the door, locks it, and says 'There!'"

I don't know what to say. I feel that the policeman is just behind me waiting to seize me, to drag me through the streets with all my friends looking on—Herr Senger too, and the Lord God who has come to life again. Then he will slam the door of the lock-up and say, "There!" and go away leaving me alone in the dark.

I'm frightened; I want to hide.

"I shall run away into the forest," I cry, "and never come back again."

"Why don't you play with us any more?" Frieda asks.

"Because I don't want to."

"Oh, come on!"

Frieda takes my hand. It is summer and holiday

time. We walk away from the town and steal some apples from Mannheim's garden. Then we run into the fields, where the rye smells like newly baked bread. We hide ourselves in the rye, and Frieda nestles up to me, and I take her in my arms just like the grown-ups, and kiss her mouth.

"Oh, dear," says Frieda, "now I shall have a baby."

When Frieda comes the next day she says:

"I've got the baby."

"Has it come already?" I ask.

"Don't be so silly! It's in my stomach; I can see it there. It's big as this"—she spreads her arms to show how big it is.

"But it's bigger than you," I exclaim, shocked.

Then Frieda runs away; but next day I call on her.

"Has it come yet?"

"No, I think it will come tomorrow."

"Does your father know?"

"I shan't tell him. He sent Anna away when she had a baby."

Early next morning I am standing outside Frieda's house, whistling for her to come. Frieda comes to the window, sees me, puts out her tongue at me and disappears. I go on waiting; but when Frieda comes out she passes me without a word. The baby is forgotten.

When I am nine I leave the elementary school and go to Father Kusch's school for boys. Stanislaus never comes to see me now.

"You're too good for me," he says, "and anyway your father's a town councilor now. That's nearly as good as being Kaiser. Good-by."

We used to play with everybody, but now we look down on all the poor children who go to the elementary school and don't learn Latin.

Father Kusch interrupts the lesson every ten minutes.

"It's my heart," he says, taking a long drink from a medicine bottle.

But we soon discover that it's not medicine in the bottle, but schnapps. One day he forgets to put his bottle away, and we pour out the schnapps and fill it with water.

"It's my heart," explains Father Kusch, but when he drinks he makes a frightful face and jumps up seizing his cane. There's nothing wrong with his heart now, and we have to hold out our hands to be caned—all except Helmut, who has brought him a chicken.

"You certainly can't have had anything to do with this, Helmut," he says.

There is a pond at the back of the school, and in winter we slide on the ice before we go into school. In one place there is a straw bundle stuck up on a stick to show where the ice is thin.

"Keep away from there!" I shout to Max. But it is too late; Max is already up to his chest in the cold water. I run to help him, but he pulls me into the water too. However, with a great effort, I manage to pull him out. Father Kusch makes me go home to change my wet clothes, and then I am to go to Herr Sel, Max's father.

"Give me my cane!" cries Herr Sel. Max has to stay in bed all the next day—which is the Kaiser's birthday and a holiday. I go to see him, and find his aunt has left a box of chocolates with "For the life-saver" written on it. Max looks sulkily at the chocolates, then at me.

"I could have got out all right without you," he says. "You shan't have more than half of them."

In the afternoon Mother sends me to the hall where the burgomaster and the town councilors and the War League are celebrating the Kaiser's birthday. Father is very proud of me, and presents me to the burgomaster.

"Our little hero," says the burgomaster.

I answer: "Max says he could have got out without me." And when it is all over I throw away the chocolates.

Grown-ups are our enemies; Julie, our old cook, is the only one who understands at all. To her I recite my first poem, which was made up on a ride through the cherry country. I was sitting next to the driver. All the rest of the children were happy and singing, but I wasn't singing. I was unhappy. I enjoyed driving as a rule, but I didn't want to take the reins then. Neither the sun nor the spring air could rouse me. I was full of a bitter-sweet sadness, and in all that blueness and sunshine my thoughts were of ravens, gloomy darkness, and death.

I read the poem to Julie, who weeps with emotion.

"Would you like an omelette," she asks, "or a chop?"

"I am going to write a story, Julie, and it will be acted in Berlin and you shall sit in the Royal Box."

Julie won't tell anybody how old she is. When you ask her she crosses herself and says: "Nobody in the world has ever known how old I am."

She has a sweetheart, a tailor in Margonin; but really he exists only in her imagination; he was invented for her by one of Father's friends. But the human heart is greater than a lie. Julie loves her sweetheart, even though she has only seen him once. The stranger who is unwittingly cast for this rôle knows nothing of the love he has awakened; but Julie believes in him utterly. The grown-ups forget the joke soon enough; but to me it is all quite real. I write the most beautiful love-letter and take it to Julie, and read it to her. I join in her praises of her sweetheart's faithfulness; I lament with her the fate that keeps him so far away; and we both give vent to our hatred of those who so cruelly thwart their happiness. Julie is blissfully happy, and I share in her happiness. Other people laugh; but I don't laugh now. I get angry when they mock at Julie.

"Don't you answer them when they ask you about

your sweetheart," I say to Julie, "or else pull their legs; tell them he has gone to America."

I get even more omelettes than before, but it is not because of the omelettes that I play at being Julie's go-between. Before long I am dissatisfied with this sweetheart for being an ordinary tailor, making suits for clerks and shopkeepers. I make him join the army, and in a few weeks he is promoted to be Lieutenant; soon he becomes Major and then General. Julie believes it all; Julie who is the terror of butchers who try to pass off brisket for sirloin; Julie who watches over her fowls with an eagle eye, marshaling the lazy ones into the stable and shooing away the broody hens. In due course the General is ennobled; and finally he chooses a distant land, which I call Mariko, to rule over as King. An underground road reached by steps invisible to me and unknown to everybody else connects our house with the capital of Mariko. The King is a very good man. He conquers the heathen and baptizes them. But the wars never last very long; they last just as long as my appetite for Madeira cake. I go to Julie in the kitchen, and shut the door.

"A telegram, your Majesty!"

"Read it," says Julie, drying her hands on her apron.

"Beloved Juliana," I read, "I have slain the heathen in bloody conflict, and weary of the heat of battle I long for a cake from your hand. Bake a good

Madeira cake at once and give it to my minister, Ernst, to send to me."

Silently Julie goes to the store-cupboard and takes out eggs, sugar, and flour and silently mixes them.

No reproaches from my mother can stop her.

She limps over to the hearth; her large face with its fleshy nose and high cheekbones and watery-blue eyes is red in the firelight, and her thin blond hair, tightly screwed back, glistens with its fragrant oil. I take the Madeira cake and bow deeply; in the nursery my friends the Marikonians are waiting, and we consume the cake on behalf of our king.

A queen must wear orders, so I steal some paper cotillion favors from my sister and sew them on to a sofa cushion; then I wind a handkerchief round Father's walking stick and use the decorated stick for a sword. I lead Julie to the Christmas tree and tell her in solemn tones to kneel before me, and I strike her shoulder with my sword: the accolade. Now she is a knight, and I present her with orders from the Pope and the King. When my father asks Julie if she really received the accolade, she says: "Yes, and didn't he give me a whack too!" She refuses with pride and scorn the thousand marks which Herr Müller offers her for one of her orders.

One day Julie falls ill; Julie who has never had a day's illness in her life; who has always been used to looking after the sick, Mother, Father, and the children; who has never feared infection and has watched at our bedsides night after night. The doctor can do nothing for her. In her illness Julie does not realize that her end is near. She goes on working as she has always worked her whole life long. "Frau Toller, what are you doing in the kitchen?" she asks. "I can manage by myself, thank you." She cooks and roasts, scolds the lazy servant girl, and runs out to the coach to put a rug round Father's feet so that he shan't catch cold. Thus she died.

After her death we find all her belongings in various boxes and chests. She has not saved any money, but she has dozens of stockings, dozens of cotton vests, dozens of flannel petticoats, dozens of jackets and blouses, all bought for her trousseau. It was her wish to be buried as a virgin in her bridal robes with a myrtle wreath on her brow and the priest walking before her coffin. And on her grave-stone she wished carved: "Here lies Juliana Jungermann, virgin."

Julie had saved nothing. Only Mother knew that she was not a virgin, and had a son. She writes to the son, and he comes to the funeral, a big portly man following the coffin in which Julie lay in peace, though without her myrtle wreath. He counts the stockings, the petticoats, the vests, the blouses, the jackets, and packs them all up in a great chest and goes away with them. But the priest, who knew Julie, is touched, and walks before the coffin and blesses the dead woman, and extols her virtue.

The boys' school gradually dwindles until I am the only pupil left, and Father Kusch teaches me in his own home. His heart is much worse, and the little medicine bottle has given place to a large bottle of schnapps.

Then I go to the *Realgymnasium* in Bromberg, the capital of the district. First I board with Herr Freundlich, one of the masters; later with Frau Ley, a doctor's wife. She is divorced from her husband, but when he is made Sanitary Officer she begins to wonder whether she shall participate in his glory and have her name-plate changed. Playing the piano is considered an accomplishment, and I have lessons from the celebrated Herr Spielmann. He is quite pleased with me, but I am only allowed to practice between five and six, and this limitation so annoys me that I give up the piano.

I write still more poems, and they sound a rebellious note; one of them begins:

"Awake, awake! Arise!
Ye that bow a coward's head,
Ye that fear the tyrant's eye,
Dare ye call this life then free?
Arise, take arms, defend yourselves
And 'gainst the bloody tyrant rise;
Spurn him 'neath your conquering feet,
And freedom's wreath shall crown your brow."

I get fifty pfennigs a week pocket money, but apple tarts with whipped cream cost twenty pfennigs each, and I like to have them every day. So I send news of my home town to the *Ostdeutsche Rundschau* in

33

Bromberg. I get paid two pfennigs a line. It is not difficult to expand the news. I take paragraphs from the *Samotschiner Zeitung*, pad them out with adjectives and alter the figures. For instance, when one of Farmer Nowak's oxen is struck by lightning and killed, I report the terrible death of half a dozen oxen. I enjoy writing; I polish the phrases; soon I am changing not the figures but the verbs and adjectives, and I spend hours bettering sentences that do not please me.

Herr Grun, the tinker, sells his plot of land to a Pole, and I wax highly indignant. I hold forth about Grun's lack of patriotism; I demand intervention by the Prussian authorities; what times we live in, I write, when morals and common decency are daily flouted and Germans are no longer on the alert. What will become of the Fatherland?

I go home for the holidays. I get out of the train at Weissenhöhe, and there is our carriage to meet me. On the outskirts of Samotschin I find Julius waiting for me. "Schramm's cow has calved," he calls out. He refuses to come into the carriage, but runs alongside, announcing to all and sundry that Toller's Ernst is home again.

How often have I been beastly to Julius! How often have I run after him with the other children crying "Dirty little Rawitsch pauper!"

Julius is an orphan and half mad: every day he is

invited to eat by a different family, and Rawitsch is the prison town.

The harshest treatment cannot put him off, he remains my friend in spite of everything; he remains everybody's friend, although they all make fun of him. Now that Samotschin has a railway station of its own, he meets every train. If a Catholic priest alights, Julius, in an effort to be kind, will bow and wave his hand toward the town and say: "All Catholics here."

One evening some farmers invite him to drink with them; they want to see what he is like when he is drunk. But when he falls down in an epileptic fit, foaming at the mouth, they leave him where he lies. Julius dies. The news of his wretched death spreads through the whole town.

That night I cannot sleep. It is the first time that I have come face to face with the cruelty of the world, and I cannot understand the ways of humanity; men could be good with so little trouble, yet they delight in evil. In the morning I write a paragraph for the *Samotschiner Zeitung*:

"Last week Julius, a workman, died. From three o'clock to half past nine he lay in convulsions at the railway station without a soul going to his aid or calling in a doctor. Have things gone so far that a dying man is to be left lying for street urchins to pelt with stones? When the police were informed of his condition their attitude was that it was nothing to do with them, since he was lying in the territory of the Prussian State Rail-

35

way. How can men cling so blindly to the letter of the law when a man's life is at stake? The man's whereabouts was beside the point; it did not matter in the least whether he was lying on State property or any other property. It is said that Julius did not deserve any special consideration. But the fact remains that had it been an animal in distress, and not a man, help would have been immediately forthcoming."

Herr Knaute, the editor, is very pleased with this.

But the burgomaster, imagining that his enemies were behind this attack, feels himself threatened and insulted, and in the next issue inserts the following paragraph, paid for with taxpayers' money:

"Warning. If the anonymous author of 'A Letter to the Editor' does not reveal his identity within three days he will be sued for libel."

"Didn't I tell you that anonymity always does the trick? You lie low," says Herr Knaute.

When the three days are up the burgomaster issues a summons against "a person unknown," and Herr Knaute is subpoenaed.

"I am a journalist," he says, "and I will never give away any colleague of mine. I can only say that he is a Jew."

Herr Knaute was fined thirty marks for refusing evidence.

"I have not betrayed you," he says to me. "I am a man of my word, and you can rely on me. Pay

the thirty marks to me direct, will you? I must have it by tomorrow."

Thirty marks! Where am I to find thirty marks? If I don't produce them Herr Knaute will reveal my name and I shall be expelled from school as a result of the scandal. The interest of the people is by now thoroughly aroused, and everybody is following the case with intense excitement. The cowardly burgomaster refuses to move without a police escort. Then by some accident—I had not said anything—my father discovers that I am the author of the paragraph. He says nothing to me about it, but goes straight to the burgomaster. He is a town councilor, and that very day the burgomaster withdraws his action.

I am glad, and angry too, when the action is dropped. I know that the burgomaster only withdrew because I am the son of a town councilor, and I realize for the first time that even the power of authority has its limits.

There is hardly anyone at Julius' funeral, only children and idiots mostly. One of the idiots is Louis, and at the funeral the children stop teasing him for once. Louis is our street-sweeper. It has always been a great grief to him that he has to cart away his rubbish in a two-wheeled handcart; he is always petitioning the council to vote him a proper cart, but he never gets it. At last, however, he gets a three-wheeled handcart, which is the apple of his eye. He calls it his "wagon," but the children still shout after him:

"There's Louis with his go-cart!"

At this Louis stops work and curses them. Then with desperate seriousness and a shaking voice he tries to convince the children that he is no longer what he used to be, that his whole life has changed, that he is no longer pushing a two-wheeled handcart; that God had not passed him by, and soon everyone will realize it.

One of my father's friends has invited me to his estate to shoot partridge, snipe and hare.

"Did you shoot a stag yesterday?" Herr Schauer asks me.

That frightens me. I had seen a stag and aimed at it, but realized that I had no buckshot, only small shot, in my gun; then in a sudden overwhelming wave of excitement I had fired. The animal had run away.

"Did you shoot a stag yesterday?" Herr Schauer asks again.

"Yes," I mutter.

"With buckshot?"

"No."

"Come and look. Your stag is lying in the glade. You will never shoot a stag with small shot again."

I go to the glade, and as I approach the stag it stands up and hobbles away a few paces and then collapses. The dumb accusation of those great moist brown eyes haunts me. I know now that I will never use a gun again.

The masters of the *Gymnasium* never speak to the masters of the *Realgymnasium* unless they are first spoken to. Even the girls prefer to flirt with the boys from the *Gymnasium*.

In the *Gymnasium* you learn both Greek and Latin, in the *Realgymnasium* only Latin. The *Gymnasium* is regarded as the sacred temple of the classical ideal, whereas the *Realgymnasium* prepares you for practical life.

Preparation for practical life is called mathematics. We learn formulæ which we do not understand and soon forget. We learn history for the sake of dates. It is quite unimportant to see the history of the world in proper perspective, to understand the relation of cause and effect; but it is of the greatest possible importance that we should know the dates of battles and coronations. Napoleon was a thief who robbed Germany of her treasures, taking even the tiles from the roofs of the churches. If you do not answer the master's questions in that spirit you are a marked man, and will come to a bad end. The masters give us the same subjects for essays that they were given when they were at school, time-honored phrases, rusty with age. And woe betide the pupil who brings his own original ideas to them. Henceforward he is a suspected person, a revolutionary. He must learn the fear of God, he must learn submission and obedience.

One day I am a bad pupil, the next day good. If I like the master I work hard; if I don't like him I am lazy. I am still troubled by thoughts of God; the boy killed Him, but the youth seeks Him with all the strength of his awakening intellect. I harass the master with all sorts of questions; I ask him to explain the legendary miracles of the Bible. "If there were only two people at the beginning of the world," I say, "Adam and Eve, then their children, the brothers and sisters, must have married each other." But he won't answer my question, punishes me for asking it and calls me a stiff-necked little atheist. I am bored with writing essays, and write to a place in Leipzig which supplies school essays at twenty pfennigs a page.

All the books I like best are banned in the school: Hauptmann and Ibsen, Strindberg and Wedekind.

We have a literary society called Clio. Professor Thiene, the headmaster, learns that I have read a scene from *Rose Bernd* to the society. He summons me to his study. "Gerhart Hauptmann," he says, "is an ultra-modern revolutionary. I forbid such readings. Go back to your mathematics; you will find that they are far more important when you leave school." But I have other plans for my future. I write poems, tales, and plays. I send the plays to the Bromberg Municipal Theatre, and when I get no reply I feel myself very much unappreciated. I want to be an actor; I play all the big parts in the school performances. I am Tiberius in Geibel's *Death of Tiberius,* and die with resonant pathos.

In the holidays I am sent to a little place in Rügen, but I don't stay there long. I take the steamer to

Denmark and roam about the country. Standing by Hamlet's legendary grave, I waver, just as he did, between the impulse toward action and the longing for death, and when I am back again at school next term I feel fettered and imprisoned.

I want to be a farmer; I dream of the simple life alone with the changing seasons. Then I forget the dream and determine to try one more year at school. I am tortured by this indecision; everybody knows what they want to do except myself.

My father is dying. I am with him when he dies. His hands grope blindly over the counterpane, his eyes are unseeing, his breath is labored; he tries to get up, and I hold him down in the bed.

"It's your fault," he groans, "it's your fault."

"Father!" I cry in horror.

Mother comes in.

"Fetch the doctor!" she cries.

The death rattle begins and I rush out of the room. When I return Mother is wringing her hands in grief and sobbing tearlessly.

She binds a cloth round my father's head and chin; she closes his eyes, and then sits down at the bedside. And when she looks at him, so rigid there, at last she begins to cry.

I lie in bed and freeze. The cold creeps up my legs. I cannot forget those words, those last words that my father cried out as he died; I shall never forget them, although I know they were spoken in delirium. I only wish Father could listen to me just once again; I want to tell him that it wasn't my fault, it was the cancer. But Father will never speak again, he is cold, and his nose is sharp. Soon I shall never see him again. That is death.

A German battleship has suddenly appeared at Agadir, and everybody is talking about war between France and Germany. The old masters warn us in confidence against the French master, who is an exchange teacher. Every Frenchman is a spy, they say, and the most inoffensive ones are the most cunning. We must not answer any questions. Monsieur reports every word we say to Paris.

All my friends hope there will be war. The masters tell us that peace breeds softness, but war a race of heroes. We long for adventure, and think that perhaps we shall escape the last year at school; perhaps we shall all be in uniform tomorrow. What a life that would be! But peace is preserved, the masters forget their militarism, and we don't escape a single hour of school.

The door slams behind her. I hear the metallic rattle of the key. I emerge from the doorway in which I have been taking shelter and cross the road to stare up at the familiar second floor window. She must be at the first floor by now; in the darkness of the corridor her hand will be seeking the curve of the banisters, her feet will be feeling for the steep, worn tread of the stairs which lead to the second story. A patch of yellow light appears on the black blind, and then a slim silhouette is framed by the window, as she draws the light curtains. The ray of light disappears, the empty window stares blackly back at the darkness.

Eighteen-years-old goes home.

She has been acting for a month now at the Bromberg Municipal Theatre. I saw her first in *Everyman*. When she came on in a white dress which fell to her feet in heavy folds, I hung over the edge of the gallery and saw her only, heard only her words, had no eyes for anything else.

Every day I sit in the little tea-shop opposite the theater and wait for her. Then I follow her in silence to the familiar house in the Danzigerstrasse.

Two months later my landlady, Frau Möller, says: "Maria Gross has just been here; she wants the room next to yours."

But she does not take it. Next time I meet her, on the impulse of the moment I raise my hat.

Then one day she speaks to me.

She tells me that she is the illegitimate daughter of an actress, which is a disgrace. I reply to her that there is no question of disgrace, that on the contrary many legitimate children are a disgrace. She says: "You are trying to console me." I reply: "I am not, indeed. I swear it's the truth." After that we meet every day. I tell Maria about my poems, and I can't resist the temptation of reading some of them to her.

"They're splendid," she says. "The cadences remind me of Schiller. I'll read one of them at the charity dinner of the Horse Grenadiers, although my father was not in the cavalry."

One day she announces that she has a fiancé.

"Do you love him?"

"He's too exhausting," she says. "He is an actor."

"He's a blackguard. I'll kill him if ever I lay hands on him!"

Maria gets up, comes and sits down beside me on the sofa, and leans her head on my chest. I want to kiss her, but she is a saint, and one does not kiss saints; if I kiss her now she will come to think that I also am "too exhausting," like that blackguard of a fiancé. I swear to myself never to kiss her. I will rescue her.

I write a letter to her mother.

"Dear Madam, put your trust in me. Your daughter has fallen into the clutches of a villain. I love your daughter. But you must not think ill of me for that. I am only young, but in a few weeks' time I shall be taking my final examination. And then I will deliver your daughter from the hands of her seducer."

Maria's mother replies:

"Young man, it is very nice to hear that you love my daughter. But my daughter can look after herself. Do well in your examination, and forget my daughter. Do this for the sake of Maria's unhappy mother."

Maria is bored with me. When I call on her the landlady says that Maria is studying and must not be

44

disturbed. On the second day of the examination there is a solicitor's letter on the breakfast table. I open it and read that I have insulted the actor X by calling him a blackguard, that the actress Maria Gross will bear witness to this, and that I am summoned to appear at the police court in a fortnight's time.

I go back to my room and seize the knife with which I had intended to kill the actor. She shall see how deeply I have loved her. If this case gets to court it will be good-by to all my chances in the examination.

My uncle, the solicitor, laughs.

"I'll offer your actor fifty marks, and he'll soon stop feeling insulted."

In spite of the bad work I did on the second day I succeed in my examination.

The actor's honor cost twenty-five marks more than my uncle thought.

On the school notice-board there is an alluring prospectus of the University of Grenoble. I will go to France and Maria can go to blazes.

2. A Student in France

I went to the University at Grenoble. When they addressed me as "Monsieur" I felt like some adventurer landed on a strange island after a long voyage. Every mademoiselle was an exotic princess, mysterious and inscrutable. I frequented the bars and drank absinth which I didn't like, and generally regarded myself as a devil of a fellow. I sat for hours in the cafés, and was deeply impressed by the fact that everybody kept their hats on; so I kept mine on too, and thought to myself, So this is the wicked *Grande Nation!*

There was a Russian girl living in my pension, the daughter of a minister; she was extremely ugly, but that didn't matter; the point was that she was a Russian, probably a Nihilist, who knew all about bombs, and would return one day to her peasants. One day, I thought, I shall read how she has assassinated a terrible Grand Duke. In the next room to mine was an Austrian ex-officer, who had a mistress, a little French dressmaker. It was he who taught me the A B C of the man of the world. "Be careful with these girl students," he said, "they don't stop philosophizing even in bed, and anyway they're no virgins. If you want to know what's what, you must go to the brothel. The proprietress is a real woman of the world. She drives a carriage with two thoroughbred arabs, and has an account with the Crédit Lyonnais. She's a bit of a philosopher and understands life; and if she likes the look of you she'll give you credit."

But I preferred to spend my time in the German Students' Union. We used to discuss Nietzsche and Kant, and sitting upright on our stools we drank glass after glass of light beer with our elbows high and our chests stuck out in order "to feel at home." We deprecated the smuttiness of the French, and preened ourselves on being pioneers of a loftier culture. To bring the evening to a close we would open the window and sing *Deutschland, Deutschland über alles, über alles in der Welt* at the top of our voices. The townsfolk would gather in the square below and listen to our songs, and shake their heads and laugh. None of us would ever go home alone, we always walked in twos, for we were in the country of the "hereditary foe," and one never knew: we won the war of 1870-71 and we seized Alsace-Lorraine, and the *Revanche* might come at any time. There were women in our Union as well as men; elderly school-mistresses given six months' leave to learn to speak French like a native. They never did; they were too proud. They wore "sensible" dresses and broad hygienic shoes, and warned us of the easy morals of

47

this degenerate nation, and exhorted us never to forget that as Germans we had a special mission.

I rarely went to the University. The lectures bored me, and most of the professors reminded me of shop-walkers: they praised the various aspects of the official culture in phrases that sounded like advertising slogans. Grenoble is a regular French propaganda factory.

I was really living in France without ever having left Germany. I lived and moved among Germans —in the University, at lunchtime, in the cafés, and every evening. I forgot even my scanty school-French. But after a time I determined to cut out the Union. The Austrian ex-officer asked me whether I played cards. I couldn't, but I went with him: perhaps card-playing was the best way to learn French.

We used to meet every afternoon in a café, students from all over Europe. We played a game called "Bank of Poland" which had nothing to do with either banks or Poland. Gold and silver changed hands with restless frequency. We used to drink black coffee, and it was all very jolly. One day I sat watching the players. The little French dressmaker sat next to me, and the Austrian officer lost one twenty-franc piece after another. The little dressmaker smiled at me, and my knee brushed against hers. She stood up, and I followed her. She asked me where I lived. She must have known, but perhaps she had forgotten; she wanted to see my room and called me *mon petit*. I glanced down at the Austrian

48

and saw that he was still losing. She slipped her arm through mine, I was very happy; I learned French.

The Austrian lost still more on the following day. I had to lend him money. The girl had to sit behind him with her hand on his left shoulder. But he went on losing all the same, and exclaimed angrily that he was only losing because I refused to play. So I put down five francs, and won. The girl stealthily put her other hand on my right shoulder, and I put down ten francs and won again. The right shoulder was luckier than the left. I put down twenty francs again and again, until I had a pile of money in front of me. The officer did not notice that the girl had taken her hand from his shoulder and was holding it out to me; for I had begun to lose. I filled it with gold pieces without looking at her and went on losing. The waiter pushed back the table, for it was midnight and the landlord wanted to close down. I had lost all the money for my rent and my fees, except for twenty francs. The girl had taken her hand from my shoulder long ago; she had gone over to a Pole who was said to put all his winnings into French securities. Then we went on to a bar, and played still more. I began winning again. I was no longer aware of what went on about me and saw only the green baize of the table swimming in a green blur which blotted out everything else. I was playing to the limit, and I must have won a great deal; I felt the girl behind me again. At three in the morning the bar closed down, and somebody said: "Let's go

49

on to Madame Aline's." "Who is Madame Aline?" I asked. "She's that woman I told you about," the Austrian said.

The cold night air sobered me, and I wanted to go home. "You can't do that," said the Austrian, "not after you've won so much. And anyway you've been playing with whores for the last hour or two, and a man of the world never wins from whores. Come on to Madame Aline's, and if you go on winning there you can take it as the will of God, and bear your fate manfully."

In Madame Aline's salon there were a number of French N.C.O.s. The hereditary foe, I thought to myself. But there was no denying that they were drinking beer, and would have done credit to the German Union. Obviously one had to make exceptions. Sitting on their knees were the schoolmistresses, who were the professional *dames des salons;* they had taken off their "sensible" dresses and their hygienic sandals; they were quite naked.

Madame Aline came to welcome us. The Queen of England herself could not have greeted us more graciously. She asked us what we wanted, pitied the young ladies who would have to go without us, and invited us to share a bottle of champagne so that she could drink to our health and to the luck of the cards. I sat at the table with a heavy head, annoyed with myself for playing, and enjoying with a perverted pleasure first the loss of all my winnings, then the loss of all my possessions.

At seven o'clock, in the brilliant sunlight of the spring morning, I wandered home without a centime in my pocket and minus my watch, which I had left in pledge with the Pole. The Austrian walked at my side philosophizing over the worthlessness of the world and all earthly goods; he had won three hundred francs. By midday my stomach had begun gnawing. I told the landlady I was unwell, and would be living on tea and bread for the next few days. I discovered a few francs in the bottom of a vase and pondered on the telegram I would have to send home. I tried again and again before I could concoct a satisfactory message. Finally I settled on:

"Lent every penny to a Turk. Turk has disappeared."

The card-playing adventure gave me plenty to think about. In the sober light of day I could not understand the man who had yielded so completely to the chaotic license of night. But he was no stranger. He was myself, and nobody else. Thenceforward I would have to reckon with a new self of whose existence I had been entirely unaware. No more cards for me. I started attending lectures at the University—legal, literary, philosophical. I began to read Nietzsche, Dostoievski, Tolstoi.

At the end of June I traveled through Provence with a group of German students. "We will all drink in the South together," said one of the schoolmistresses on the eve of our departure, flourishing her

51

Baedeker. In every town she "drank in" the museums with their dubious busts and pictures, the remains of old ruins, every monument which Baedeker had starred; and we had to participate in it all, too. She found jerry-built manors picturesque and rubbishy façades bizarre. A lovely old fountain served as text for a lecture on the progress of mankind; today we had running water in every house—who could tell where we would be in fifty years' time? We ought to be proud to be alive.

I escaped from them at Nîmes and established myself in an ancient hotel where I fell in love with the landlady. The Provençals speak their own variety of French and I could scarcely understand it; they could scarcely understand me either, and I passed as a Parisian.

The landlady guessed that I was in love with her; and on the second day she asked me if I wouldn't prefer another room on the second floor. Perhaps she slept on the second floor herself and wished to be discreet. One had to bear in mind the gossip of staff and neighbors in a little town like this; there are always jealous people ready to run to the Police. One must come to some sort of compromise between harsh reality and the exquisite dream of love.

"If you think so," I answered in a low voice.

"The room has no window, I'm afraid," she said softly, "but plenty of air comes in from the corridor." She was faced with the danger of turning away an English couple, she explained, unless I took this other room; and to whom else should she turn if not to me, the Parisian, the old friend of the house?

In Marseille I stayed at a little hotel by the harbor. I met a young German in the restaurant who wanted to join the Foreign Legion. After all, why not? The Foreign Legion meant adventure; none of your heavy-headed card-playing, but Africa, deserts, lions, Bedouin, a bold life and a bold death. Adventure beckoned ever more alluringly. Gamblers I had already met; who might I not encounter now? That afternoon I unfolded my plans to a French corporal who was eating at our table. He listened to me seriously and meditatively, tapped me on the shoulder, drained his glass and said: "Get it out of your head, my lad; the Foreign Legion is no joke!"

When I stood watching the soldiers being embarked for Africa, each just a number, each just a sack to be pushed this way and that, I lost my enthusiasm for the Legion and freedom seemed suddenly a splendid thing. I was free to do what I wanted. Tomorrow I could go to Toulon, and if I didn't like Toulon I would go back to Grenoble.

It was then that I began to take stock of myself. I was a young man from a middle-class home and I had been taking all my privileges absolutely for granted. It had seemed perfectly right and natural that I should study at leisure and travel, all at my mother's expense. I had not given a thought to the idea of freedom; it was no more than a theme for lectures in philosophy. That my friend Stanislaus should have had to work for a daily wage since he was fourteen, and that on top of that he should have to help support his parents out of his meager earnings, had seemed right and inevitable, just as my freedom to enjoy life seemed right and inevitable. But suddenly and for the first time this right seemed problematical. I saw for the first time the foundations and limits of my external freedom: money. Money given me by my mother. Why did she have money, while Stanislaus' father had none? I thought of my childish question as to why Stanislaus should have to eat pickled herrings and baked potatoes while we had roast meat. And Mother's answer, "Because it's God's will," no longer satisfied me. I began to doubt the inevitability of a system in which one man can squander money senselessly while another suffers from lack of bread. But I loved money. It was to money that I owed all my delights. It was only thanks to money that I was able to laze away that radiant morning among the blossoming wistaria and feathery mimosa; that I was able to lie and listen to the Mediterranean lapping gently and rhythmically along the rocky coast. Yes, I loved money; but with a guilty conscience. The day was spoilt for me, the world was spoilt for me. Values which only yesterday had seemed eternal and unassailable now seemed questionable; I myself seemed questionable.

I was sitting in front of a lonely church near Cap Martin. I got up and went into the church, into the twilight stillness of a world where man can only achieve blessedness through faith. A few days ago I had been hankering after the Foreign Legion, and now, if a priest had only appeared and spoken the right words he would have found me ready to renounce the world. I dreamed of being received into some distant monastery, of leaving outside its walls my name and all the desires of yesterday; of taking the vows of silence and living nameless and abandoned in a world bounded by the monastery walls.

But no priest came. And outside the cool evening wind touched me into hunger. In the next village I came to I made a meal of goat's milk cheese washed down with the local sour red wine, and suffered no pangs of conscience. Outside the café the men were playing bowls, while the village girls walked up and down laughing and flirting; automatic machines blared forth the latest Paris songs, and the stars shone large and serene. All conflict was forgotten, doubts and beliefs fell away, the world was so lovely.

In Sarajevo the heir to the Austrian throne was murdered. The Austrian and Serbian students were at once recalled. I accompanied an Austrian friend to the station, and when he said: *"Auf Wiedersehen,"* I didn't know what to answer; I could not rid myself of the thought that perhaps in a year he would be dead. I went home, and those four letters, D, E, A, D, rang through my head, I could not get rid of them. I met them everywhere, in conversation, in the newspapers. I saw them on a placard summoning the Socialist workers of Grenoble to a great anti-war demonstration. In the evening I went to this mass meeting, and stood wedged in a jam of French workers, men and women. I watched their honest, good-tempered faces, whose clear, simple lines grew tense and hard when the speaker denounced war. No, these people certainly didn't want war. Their cry, "*Vive la paix!*" was a war-cry against war.

The Austro-Serbian war came. Morning, noon and night the papers were full of news from the battle-fields; we became used to it and once more cherished the foolish hope that the war could be confined to Austria and Serbia. At the end of July the University closed for the long vacation. I wanted to go to Paris and take a course in French at the Sorbonne. On the eve of my departure I sat drinking an apéritif in a café, and suddenly the place was filled with a mob of newsboys: "Late night special! Jaurès assassinated." Everyone began talking in excited groups, and I heard one worker say to another: "*C'est la guerre.*" In the café, outside the café, in all the streets and parks people talked excitedly together. When at midnight the usual cannon shot was fired from the fortress the people scattered in a sudden panic.

The nearest German Consul was at Lyons, and I wanted to ask him whether or not I ought to go to Paris. On July 31st I was on my way to Lyons. Every station was thick with soldiers, men on leave being recalled to their regiments. In Lyons I asked the Consul:

"Will it be all right for me to go to Paris?"

"Why not?"

"You don't think there is any danger of war?"

"Rubbish!"

"It's not just for myself that I'm asking. The German students at Grenoble are wondering what they ought to do."

"Get on with their work," said the Consul.

A few hours later the newsboys were shouting:

"Mobilization in Germany."

One late night special after another.

"State of war declared in Germany!"

"Mobilization in Germany!"

"French border violated by German soldiers!"

And still I met processions of workers crying: "*A bas la guerre!*" And still I saw the Socialist papers, black-bordered in mourning for Jaurès. But now the die was cast. The smell of war was in the air.

"Germany's ultimatum to France!" yelled the newsboys. Their papers were torn from their hands.

"They want war!" screamed a woman's voice. "They want war!"

A great crowd was seething in the Place Bell-cour. Orators climbed up onto the pedestal of the statue.

"France is threatened," one shouted. "Her freedom is at stake."

"No, not her freedom but her glory," cried another.

"To hell with glory—it's Alsace-Lorraine that's at stake," cried a third.

"*Vive l'Alsace-Lorraine*," the crowd shouted.

But no orator found such favor as one who reminded his audience of the Revolution, of France's historical mission to free Prussia from militarism and bring democracy to Germany.

"It's not the Germans we hate," he cried, "it's their Kaiser!"

Resounding applause.

A woman jumped up next to the speaker. "When we get to Berlin we'll clip the Kaiser's whiskers!" she cried. And the crowd roared in chorus: "*Coupez la barbe de Guillaume!*"

Processions of youth marched through the streets pounding out a song with heavy-footed rhythm. It had only one line which they repeated endlessly, fanatically:

"*Conspuez Guillaume, conspuez Guillaume, conspuez!*"

I had only one desire: to get back to Germany. At the station they told me there was a train leaving at two o'clock that night for the Swiss border. I went into a little café and waited. The war was the sole topic of conversation at all the tables. At the next table a fat sergeant was sitting, his eyes red and swollen. He sang the first words of the *Marseillaise* in a husky voice, broke off, drained his glass, and began again. Nobody paid any attention. He stood up, went to the telephone, and bawled out at the top of his voice:

"Germany has declared war on France!"

Everyone in the café was suddenly still; the sergeant returned to his table, and sat down heavily. The silence was like a darkness which absorbed all light and all humanity. The sergeant jumped up again and started singing the *Marseillaise*, and this time everybody joined in. I sat at my table, an isolated stranger; I felt a lump in my throat; never was I so afraid for Germany as at that moment. I paid and hurried out. Near the station I heard the dull tramping of horses. In the distance a black mass appeared and grew larger every minute. Trumpets blared, faces peered from every window. "The Cuirassiers!" someone yelled. And to the strains of *Sambre et Meuse* the Cuirassiers filed by.

The station was swarming with soldiers and their wives and children. They were bound for the Italian border. Italy, Germany's official ally, will not stand by her for long. At last I found myself in the train, which was full of escaping Germans. Our progress was almost imperceptible. The train was always stopping, always shunting; we waited endlessly. In the morning the carriage doors were flung open, and bearded French militia ordered us out. We were herded together in the station yard to have our passports examined. The Germans were segregated. We were under arrest.

It was only fifteen miles to the border, and some

of the fellows abandoned their luggage and made a dash for it. The officer who had had us arrested was quite at sea. He had no idea what to do with us; and finally, towards evening, we were given leave to make for the border. At midnight, only a few hours before the frontier was finally closed, we arrived at Geneva, famished and tired out; but when we found ourselves on Swiss soil again we hugged one another and sang *Deutschland, Deutschland über alles.* On the other side of the platform returning Frenchmen sang the *Marseillaise.*

Outside the station a soldier was feverishly beating a little drum and announcing the Swiss mobilization.

3. War

When the train ran into Lindau and we were at last on German soil we burst once more into *Deutschland, Deutschland über alles.* We waved to the Bavarian militia who were guarding the station; they seemed a very part of the Fatherland, of home. Sweating with importance a pot-bellied Reserve-Major ran up and down, and interrupted our song with his sharp falsetto: "Nobody may leave the train."

The militia took on a less friendly aspect; they stood at the carriage doors stern and unapproachable. But at last we were allowed to get out. Our passports were examined, our luggage searched, and our enthusiasm was strangled by endless red tape. After hours of waiting we were loaded into a freight train; the trucks were labeled: "16 men or 8 horses," and rough pine planks served as seats. We had no idea where the train was going, but that did not matter; at least it was bound for a German town.

My ears were still ringing with the cries of men insisting that France had been outraged by Germany, and now I read in the German papers that Germany had been outraged by France. And I believed it. French airmen, the Chancellor had declared, had dropped bombs on Bavarian soil, and Germany had been invaded. I swallowed it all.

At the station we were given pictures of the Kaiser inscribed: "I recognize no parties; only Germany."

The Kaiser recognized no parties; there it was in black and white; all factions were to be united; everybody spoke one language; everybody defended one mother: Germany.

Whenever we crossed a bridge we had to shut the windows. "Beware of spies!" shrieked the placards. "Take care what you say!" Every minute of the journey saw us more and more suspicious. The country was supposed to be swarming with French and Russian spies. I looked covertly at my neighbor, an honest Swabian cattle dealer, whose double chins were quivering with excitement. My neighbor looked covertly at me; instinctively we avoided each other's eyes and stared down at the floor. The air was full of unbrotherly suspicion.

I decided not to go home at once. At Munich we had to leave the train in the middle of the night, so I found a hotel and determined to enlist in the morning.

But it was not as easy as all that. The barracks were overflowing with recruits, and I was rejected by both infantry and cavalry. I had to wait. No more volunteers were required. I wandered about the streets of Munich, and in the Stachusplatz I found a raging mob. Somebody had heard two women speaking French, and they were immediately surrounded and set upon. They protested that they were Germans, but it did not avail them in the least; with torn clothes, disheveled hair and bleeding faces they were taken off by the police.

I went into the English Gardens and sat down on a seat. The ancient beeches were ruffled by the breeze; German beeches—nowhere else in the world do they grow more gloriously. A haggard-faced man was sitting beside me; and to me even the enormous Adam's apple in his scraggy neck seemed lovable. But he got up and went away, to return with several others. Bewildered, I saw them pointing at me and at my hat which lay on the bench beside me so that the lining was visible with the Lyons hatter's name on it in great blue letters. I snatched it up and continued my walk, but a rapidly increasing crowd followed me, and I heard first one and then many voices crying, "A Frenchman, a Frenchman!" I thought of the "Frenchwomen" on the Stachusplatz and quickened my stride. Children were running after me, pointing at me and crying, "Frenchy! Frenchy!" Luckily I ran into a policeman, and showed him my passport, and when the crowd surrounded me he held it up for them to see. Reluctant and abusive, they gradually dispersed. That afternoon I followed a procession to the Italian Consulate. Italy must fight with us. We sang *Deutschland, Deutschland über*

63

alles, and gave three cheers for Italy and the loyalty of our ally.

Next day I tried to enlist in the artillery. The doctor shook his head as he examined me, and I was afraid of being rejected again; I said appearances were deceptive, and really I was very strong and healthy; that I must be taken; that I was determined to be taken. The doctor smiled good-humoredly and passed me.

The old and shabby uniform flapped round my arms and legs; the boots pinched and tortured my feet; but I was proud. I was a soldier at last, a privileged defender of the Fatherland. I could not tell a private from a general, so with puffed-out chest I saluted everyone I met. In the tram a beer-sodden creature offered me his cigar-case. On one side were good light cigars, on the other poisonous-looking black ones with ostentatious bands. He indicated the black ones and made me accept one. Then he cried, slapping me jovially on the shoulders: "No mercy for those bloody Frenchies! You give it 'em!" He got out at the next stop—without paying his fare, as the conductor noticed too late.

We were trained by elderly N.C.O.s and young subalterns. They taught us how to stand at attention and how to stand at ease. We learned that nobody can be a hero on the field of battle until he can do the goose-step in his sleep.

Twice or three times every day there was a great ringing of bells, and we were all assembled to hear

news of yet another victory. We cheered and shouted
and thought that if the troops went on like this they
would soon win the war without our help.

We left Munich in the middle of August, gar-
landed and followed by women and children. But
we were not yet bound for the front. We sat all day
in the train without the least idea of where we were
going. At one stopping place a hospital train was
standing in the next platform, and a soldier with one
leg shot away was limping about on crutches, still
dressed in his torn and blood-stained uniform. It was
my first sight of a wounded man: his face was a
muddy yellow, and his cheeks sunken; his eyes were
tired and vacant. Looking at him I was aware of a
searing pain in my breast; I was afraid. But I
was determined not to be afraid; not to flinch from
what lay ahead. I thought of Germany.

In the middle of the night a voice startled us out
of our sleep; we were crossing the Rhine. We all
jumped up and craned out of the windows; and there
below us, black and silent, flowed the Rhine. The
officers flourished their swords. "*Achtung!*" shouted
one, and another began singing *Die Wacht am Rhein*,
and then we all started singing together, beating time
with our rifles.

We were living in a state of emotional delirium.
The words "Germany," "Fatherland," "War" had
a magic power, and when we uttered them they did

not die away but seemed to soar, dazzling in the air above us, intoxicating us.

We were quartered at Bellheim in the Pfalz, near Fort Germersheim. We slept in the storeroom of a chemical factory, and the corroding smell of acid mingled with the reek of human sweat; we lay on straw and slept beneath horse-blankets. The straw soon became sodden and filthy with the mud from our boots, and the blankets damp and slimy. But we did not grumble; the harder the better, we thought; the fellows in the trenches hadn't even a roof over their heads, and every hardship we suffered seemed to bring us nearer to them. Everyone rushed to volunteer when there was any dirty work to be done. When I had to clean out the stinking latrines I felt positively distinguished. There was plenty of food; too much, in fact. Every day the refuse bins were full of stale bread and lumps of fat.

The officers were hard put to it to find any use for our enthusiasm. We were drilled endlessly and sense-lessly. When it had been raining and the parade ground was sodden the N.C.O.s enjoyed themselves particularly. "Lie down!" they yelled in gloating tones. "Get up!" "Lie down!" "Get up!" We flung ourselves down into the mud, stood up, flung ourselves down again; we had to lie there with our heads in the slush, so that by the time we were dismissed we were wet through and caked with mud, and on the march back to quarters the Sergeant-Major ordered us to sing *Wie ein stolzer Adler*.

When somebody applied for fresh straw his application was refused. It was only when the bugs made sleep impossible and drove the men to scratch themselves even on parade that the doctor declared we were all lousy and the straw must be burned and the whole room disinfected.

We left the Pfalz in January, 1915. Before our departure the C.O. addressed us. Where we were going, he said, we would still be on German soil, but the place was alive with suspicious persons, enemies almost, against whose machinations we must guard ourselves. We would be billeted in private houses, but we must not trust the householders; we must lock our doors at night and sleep with our weapons beside us.

The C.O. referred to Alsace-Lorraine, which for forty-three years had been a part of Germany.

As members of the First Battalion of Heavy Artillery we were billeted in the villages round Strassburg. I was quartered in an inn where the landlord was fighting on the Eastern Front in France; it was being run by his wife and his daughter. They looked after me well, and kept me supplied with good food and wine, but I was full of suspicion. The first evening I locked my door and loaded my rifle. I dreamed that the two women broke into my room and that the old lady cut my throat with a kitchen knife while her daughter held me down. I started awake with a cry; someone was knocking at my door. It was the old landlady wanting to know whether I would like an egg for breakfast, and whether I had anything to be washed. I need not worry about anything, she said; she would look after my things. Next evening I left my door open, and my rifle unloaded. One day when I was gossiping with the daughter she complained of the suspiciousness of the officers and officials. The Alsatian soldiers were watched and spied upon, and so were the civilians. The Prussians themselves were well on the way to achieving what the French had never been able to do—breaking the bond between Germany and Alsace-Lorraine.

Our drilling went on; day after day we were told that we must have the corners knocked off us.

The advance across France had come to a standstill; nobody knew why. The papers had said nothing about our defeat at the Marne. Germany was apparently winning all along the line; nevertheless Paris remained inviolate, and the war went on.

By March our idleness had become intolerable. We did nothing half the day but stand about waiting for something to turn up. Now and then a few men were sent up to the front, and one day when the C.O. was picking three strong men for a battery in the line and had passed me by I pushed myself forward, ignoring all regulations, and asked to be taken.

"You're not strong enough," he said.

"I'm stronger than I look. I can't stand any more of this. I want to get to the front!"

The Sergeant-Major stared. The other N.C.O.s nearly burst with fury, and the C.O. looked bewildered. He hesitated, then turned on his heel and yelled to the Sergeant-Major:

"Send him up!"

4. At the Front

Our route lay through Metz. At first our conversation was loud and jerky; we would burst out suddenly into stupid remarks, silly, obscene remarks; we sat stiffly erect and stared with hard eyes into the night. We regarded ourselves as front-line men already; we played at being front-line men, opening our cartridge pouches, testing the sharpness of our bayonets, fiddling with the breech-locks of our rifles. But as time went on we lowered our voices and our words dropped heavily through the thick, stagnant air. The lights were put out and we sat in darkness as the train rumbled on through the night. We sat in silence now; our very breathing was constrained and we relaxed from our rigid poses. We had stopped playing at being front-line soldiers because for the first time we could hear the front; we were first aware of its thunder soon after leaving Metz. Then the train pulled up in the middle of nowhere and we got out onto the line where some men were awaiting us. We marched on through the night, soaked through by the rain and weighed down by our packs, until at last we came to a village. We stumped through the street, our guide knocked on a window, a door was opened, and we found ourselves in the kitchen of the battery to which we had been drafted. A fat soldier gave us hot coffee.

"Three more volunteers!" cried our guide.

"Three more bloody fools," said the cook.

I was awake before daybreak, and got up and wandered about the village, looking at the blackened walls of the shattered houses, stumbling into the shell holes which pitted the streets. The church door was open, and I went in. The dawn showed grayly through the shivered windows and my heavy boots clattered on the stone paving. A soldier was lying before the altar; when I bent over him I saw that he was dead. His head was broken clean open, and a great steel splinter was wedged between the two halves of the skull, from which the brain spilled in a pulpy mass.

Our battery was stationed halfway up the hill before Pont à Mousson. In the morning we went up loaded with hot coffee and bread for the men, whom we found sitting stripped to the waist, searching their shirts for the lice which nested in the seams.

On the way up I heard the hum of an aeroplane. I stared up curiously and saw its red, white and blue circle.

"Down on your bellies!" cried the sergeant.

There was a strange rushing, whistling sound; the aeroplane had dropped a shower of aerial darts. No one was hurt.

71

"Not one went home!" complained the guide. "The guy you're replacing had better luck. A bit of shrapnel got him while he was in the latrine, and now he's living like a duke in a hospital."

The observation post was situated in a little pocket just under the peak of the hill. With the aid of glasses I could make out the French trenches and behind them the devastated town of Pont à Mousson, and the Moselle winding its sluggish course through the early spring landscape. Gradually I became aware of details: a company of French soldiers was marching through the streets of the town. They broke formation, and went in single file along the communication trench leading to the front line. Another group followed them.

A subaltern was watching through his glasses.

"See those Frenchies?" he asked.

"Yes, sir."

"Let's tickle 'em up!"

"Range twenty-two hundred," he cried to the telephonist.

And "Twenty-two hundred," echoed the telephonist.

I kept my eyes glued to the glasses. My head was in a whirl, and I was trembling with excitement, surrendering to the passion of the moment like a gambler, like a huntsman. My hands shook and my heart pounded wildly. The air was filled with a sudden high-pitched whine, and a brown cloud of dust dimmed my field of vision.

The French soldiers scattered, rushed for shelter, but not all of them. Some lay dead or wounded.

"Direct hit!" cried the subaltern.

The telephonist cheered.

I cheered.

Every morning at eleven o'clock a dozen shrapnel shells came sailing over our battery. We were quite used to them. We knew the identity of the enemy battery which used us for target practice; and we replied in kind exactly an hour later. One day at five to eleven Josef said:

"They'll be coming over in a minute."

"Get out," we said, "there's plenty of time; another five minutes yet." And we went into the dugout to play tarot. The French shooting did our guns no harm, and ours did theirs no harm either; the daily ceremony was just an indication that the war was still on, that they were still there and we were still here. We waited in the dugout. Eleven o'clock, two minutes past, ten minutes past.

"King," said Alois. "Ace," said I. "Trump," said Josef. But he did not pick up the cards. "Why the bloody hell don't the blighters shoot?" he cried. "Their clock's stopped," said Alois. And we went on playing silently for ten minutes more.

Then a shell burst twenty yards away.

"About time too!" cried Alois. "Trump!"

Another shell burst.

Alois threw down his cards. "Something's wrong!" he cried. "That's not our little friend!"

A splinter screamed past the dugout door.

The telephone rang.

"All out into the gallery!"

We rushed into the gallery which was tunneled away from the dugout into the hillside. There was only a foot of earth over our heads, covered with beams and corrugated iron. A direct hit would have blown us all to smithereens. But this absurd tunnel gave us a vague illusion of safety as we listened to the rain of splinters rattling above our heads.

Our veteran regular, a laborer from Berchtesgaden, pulled out his rosary and started praying under his breath. Franz broke into a *Schnadahupferl*, one of the folk-songs of his home.

Then the whole hillside was shaken by a deafening explosion; it was our second ammunition dump going up. Sebastian stopped praying and Franz stared up at the roof. For two hours the bombardment went on over our heads, and the suspense was paralyzing. No orders came through from the observation post; probably the telephone wire had been shot away.

At last our heavy guns began to reply.

"Two volunteers to go up," called the N.C.O. Josef and I scrambled up the slope. Shrapnel and splinters screamed about us; but we reached the observation post at last. The enemy's fire was slackening. Now and again a shell burst and flung up the earth on our hillside, sending up columns of brown

74

dust and filling the air with flying metal. When we came to our battery we stared at the damage.

"Bloody hell!" said Josef.

"War," said Josef.

At last we found ourselves back at rest camp. It was weeks since I had taken off my uniform; weeks since I had been able to clean myself. But I soon got a bucket of water, tore off my clothes and soaped myself all over, scrubbing away ecstatically. While I was standing there naked and snorting, Sebastian, the laborer from Berchtesgaden, came up. He was a devout Catholic, and could not understand the frenzy of this war. When he received parcels of ham and bacon from home he would go into a corner and sit with his bent back against the wall and eat and stare and think. Perhaps the Prussians were to blame for it, he would think; that was more than likely. They didn't know how to keep their mouths shut. Old Bismarck had let down Bavaria properly, but old grandfer took six Prussians prisoner single-handed. "Up with your hands!" he'd shouted; "the Bavarians are here!" And now they do nothing but swill our beer in the canteen. Sebastian, seeing me, stood stock-still. He opened his eyes, took his pipe out of his mouth, and stared over my head into vacancy.

"Now I know why there's a war," he rumbled. "The Prussians wash themselves naked." He spat venomously out of the corner of his mouth.

"Prussian hog!" he shouted, went back into the dugout and peeled off his clothes in the straw.

75

The French inhabitants who lingered on in their villages in the fighting zone lived wretchedly in cellars and barns, in odd little rooms or kitchen cupboards, like shipwrecked sailors clinging to bits of wreckage, only to be swept off into eternity by a sudden storm. Impotent witness of its own downfall, the village in which parents and grandparents still lived was blown to bits, its fields plowed by guns and sown with shells instead of seed; and the fruit of the seed was death and destruction.

The French got enough from the Germans to save them from starvation; but many a woman sold herself for a loaf or a chunk of sausage. Soldiers and peasants lived together on friendly terms; they knew each other and their everyday routines and trusted each other; they shook their heads together over the war and grumbled together at idiotic orders and swore when the women were forced to do dirty work.

We need not have been afraid that there would not be anything for us to do at the front. There was no sign of the war finishing; the armies had dug themselves into the soil of France, Poland, Russia and Asia, and our men began to sing:

> "This campaign
> Is a damn slow train;
> I'll be late for my wedding
> If I don't look out."

Our Battery Commander was a medical student who had been a cadet but had been expelled from the regiment and deprived of his stripes. When the war came, however, he had been made acting First Lieutenant. His vanity, stupidity, and arrogance were the bane of our lives.

Once I failed to salute him with the requisite smartness and next day the Sergeant-Major read out the following order:

"Private Toller will report to the observation post in full marching order at 11.15 each day until further orders."

At 11.15 I was at the observation post. Lieutenant Siegel was sitting at the table, reading. I reported to Lance-Corporal Sedlmeier, and he looked through my pack.

"Your socks are not properly packed."

"Go back and put 'em right. Then report to me again," said Lieutenant Siegel softly.

I ran back down the slope, which at that time of day was always swept by shrapnel. Sweating all over I ran to earth in the dugout, rearranged my pack and tore back to the observation post.

"Where's your field dressing?"

"I must have left it behind."

"Go back and get it!" spat Lieutenant Siegel.

Sedlmeier clicked his heels and laughed ingratiatingly.

Once more I ran back to the dugout, and once more back to the observation post. I was trembling with rage.

This farce continued for three days.

77

I sat sleeplessly in my corner staring in front of me.

"I'll blow the blackguard's head off if it goes on much longer," I said aloud.

"What's he got his knife into you for?" asked Franz.

"Ask me another!"

"I know why it is. You're educated, you are; and he's afraid of you. It's always like that."

Early next morning I reported to the Major of the Bavarian troops to which our battery was attached.

"Private Toller, sir."

The Major, an energetic officer from Karlsruhe with a genial, drink-sodden face, looked at me in astonishment. I had broken all regulations in applying direct to him, and he would have to give me field punishment. I told him my trouble, and he was silent. I knew very well that he couldn't stand the pseudo-lieutenant either.

"Sit down," he said, "and have a glass of schnapps. What do you expect me to do about it?"

"I'd like a transfer, sir."

"Where to?"

"To the infantry, if possible."

"But why the infantry? What's wrong with the artillery?"

"Well, sir, we shoot, and don't know whom we're shooting at, and the others shoot back, and don't know whom they're shooting at either. I'd like to see what I'm up against."

"You're a poet?" said the Major.

"Yes, sir."

"Free verse, what? So you want a little romantic war all on your own? Your health!"

"Your health, sir."

"Have you anything particular in mind?"

"I was thinking of the machine-gun section at Bois-le-Prêtre."

"Just as you like. If you come through you must send me your new poems."

"Thank you, sir."

Two hours later the Sergeant-Major gave me formal notice of my transfer. I packed my kit, mixed the things up in a hopeless mess, and reported to Lieutenant Siegel, who received me with an oily smile.

"Shall we let bygones be bygones?" he said, and offered me his hand.

I turned abruptly.

"Halt!" he cried.

I turned round and faced him.

"Didn't you see my hand?"

"Yes, sir."

"What's the matter, then?"

"If it's an order, sir," I said, and held my hand stiffly out. His face turned dull red.

"Go to hell!"

"Thank you, sir."

A devastated wood; miserable words. A tree is like a human being. The sun shines on it. It has roots, and the roots thrust down into the earth; the rain waters it, and the wind stirs its branches. It grows, and it dies. And we know little about its growth and still less about its death. It bows to the autumn gales, but it is not death that comes then; only the reviving sleep of winter.

A forest is like a people. A devastated forest is like a massacred people. The limbless trunks stare blackly at the day; even merciful night cannot veil them; even the wind is cold and alien.

Through one of those devastated woods which crept like a fester across Europe ran the French and German trenches. We lay so close to each other that if we had stuck our heads over the parapet we could have talked to each other without raising our voices.

We slept huddled together in sodden dugouts, where the water trickled down the walls and the rats gnawed at our bread and our sleep was troubled with dreams of home and war. One day there would be nine of us, the next only eight. We did not bury our dead. We pushed them into the little niches in the wall of the trench cut as resting places for ourselves. When I went slipping and slithering down the trench, with my head bent low, I did not know whether the men I passed were dead or alive; in that place the dead and the living had the same gray faces.

Not that we always had to find a dumping place for the dead.

Often the bodies were blown to pieces, so that only

a shred of flesh sticking to a tree stump told where a man had died.

Or they rotted away in the barbed wire between the trenches.

Or if a mine blew up a section of the trench the earth was its own grave-digger.

Three hundred yards to the right of us, in that witches' cauldron, was a block-house which had been occupied twenty times by the Germans and twenty times by the French. The bodies of the dead soldiers were heaped together in one vast embrace. An appalling stench hung over them and they had been covered with a thin layer of white quick-lime.

The machine-gunners were to be withdrawn, and I was transferred to a battery east of Verdun. The green shade of ancient beeches protected us from spying aircraft; we shot and were shot at, and on the whole led a peaceful, monotonous life. The only cause for complaint was the bad food. The range-finder and the N.C.O.s had grilled steak, and filled their bellies every day. That made for bad blood. Added to that was the fact that the officer at the base had had a new mess built, while our dugout let in the water for lack of duckboards and revetting material. Also near our battery there was a new concrete dugout for the staff, complete with every comfort. "That cost twenty thousand marks," one of the builders said. "A lot of money like that ought to last more than one winter."

Latrine rumors were passing from mouth to mouth.

Soldiers had mutined in such-and-such a place, in so-and-so they had been fraternizing with the French; here they'd poured the coffee on the ground in front of a general, and there a soldier had shot an officer in the line.

The Kaiser was coming to visit the trenches, and we had to parade; the C.O. picked out the men with the cleanest uniforms for the inspection, and finally it was a little band of cooks, clerks, and such who paraded before the Kaiser and were decorated with iron crosses. Front-hogs need not apply! said the men; and the news that all guns must be unloaded and all bayonets handed in before the Kaiser appeared was received with howls of laughter.

We used to get on best with the officers who concerned themselves only with facts and necessities; but we had a bad time with the petty-minded reserve-officers who used to fuss about and take every opportunity of spying on the men, as though they felt it incumbent upon them to prove themselves lords of creation.

Once Franz's people sent him a light waterproof, and a young reserve-officer asked him who the hell he thought he was, going about in a thing like that? It was the soldier's job not to mind a bit of rain and mud; the war wasn't a joke! And anyway, if common soldiers went about in waterproofs today, to-morrow they would be parading in officers' caps!

"The officers can die like us," said Franz, "but they certainly can't live like us."

All we knew of the war was what was going on in our own little sector; for news of the other fronts we had to rely on the newspapers. Many of us indeed had no clear notion of what we ourselves had done until the papers came, when our own confused ideas were modified and often proved all wrong.

According to the newspaper feuilletons the French were a crowd of degenerates, the English a cowardly lot of shopkeepers, the Russians swine. This mania for disparging, abusing, and calumniating the enemy was so disgusting that I sent a paragraph to the *Kunstwart* deprecating an attitude which could only reflect badly on ourselves. But the editor returned it with a letter that made me despair. One had to bear in mind public opinion, he said. And thus was that public opinion bred which the men at the front came in time to spit upon.

The village A. had to be evacuated. The order came through at seven in the morning, and at seven-thirty the last inhabitant had left. When I walked through the silent streets half an hour later and wandered into houses through the open doors where there was nobody to turn me away and nobody to invite me in, I was not alone. In passage and room the air was still full of human warmth, still warm with the life of the people who had lived there until so recently. Even the lifeless objects seemed in some way still attached to their owners. Hands seemed only just raised from knob and latch; the solicitous

83

glance of the housewife seemed still to linger on china and saucepan; cupboards and chests of drawers still sheltered clothes and precious possessions; the odor of everyday life and happy hours still hung about them. The things of man part from man less readily than man parts from his things; and even when a man has long been dead his possessions remain inscrutably his.

Here the people had only left their homes because the war had driven them away; they could take no more with them than they could carry in their arms, and every room told of some painful choice. In one a woman had bundled all her bed-linen together, and then left it lying. In another a dress had been torn from the wardrobe only to be finally discarded. In another the mother or the child had collected a heap of toys and tied them up, only to abandon them at the last minute.

In the silence of this forsaken village there was nobody to question me, as I said out loud, as if one of those poor people had stood there:

"This had to be."

I hurried away. There was no one in sight; from whom was I escaping?

I was promoted to corporal. Every night I was on duty with the infantry in the trenches; we had to time the French artillery; the time between flash and detonation gave the exact distance of the battery.

We worked in three shifts: the first came on at

eight in the evening, the second at midnight, the third at four in the morning. After a few hours' sleep we left our dugout by the battery and silently plodded down the water-logged road to the wood which lay behind the third line of trenches. Around us fell the enemy shells, moaning and roaring and echoing through the night. We stumbled over tree-stumps, jumped from shell-hole to shell-hole, fell into deep pools and bogged ourselves in the mud. The shattered wood was so lit up by the bombardment that there was no knowing whether the stars were shining or whether the night was black as soot. At last we would find the communication trench, and need no longer keep our eyes glued to the ground before us.

We would shelter behind the wall of the trench and watch. Bullets sprayed up the earth into a rain of fire, ricochets screamed over our heads, Véry lights hissed quietly up and cast their pallid glare over the barbed wire of no man's land; the sounds of war mingled with the voices of the night. Far away in the distance flames would dart from the muzzles of the French artillery, and we would count the seconds that elapsed before we heard the muffled thud of the detonation. But for all these horrors the night soothed our hearts; earth and all her creatures lay under a vast and solemn veil, and our breathing was easier, our pulse quieter as, resistlessly, we were drawn into the silent stream of immutable law.

One night we heard a cry, the cry of one in excruciating pain; then all was quiet again. Someone in his death agony, we thought. But an hour later the cry came again. It never ceased the whole night. Nor the following night. Naked and inarticulate, the cry persisted. We could not tell whether it came from the throat of German or Frenchman. It existed in its own right, an agonized indictment of heaven and earth. We thrust our fingers into our ears to stop its moan; but it was no good: the cry cut like a drill into our heads, dragging minutes into hours, hours into years. We withered and grew old between those cries.

Later we learned that it was one of our own men hanging on the wire. Nobody could do anything for him; two men had already tried to save him, only to be shot themselves. We prayed desperately for his death. He took so long about it, if he went on much longer we should go mad. Death closed his mouth the third day.

I saw the dead without really seeing them. As a boy I used to go to the Chamber of Horrors at the annual fair, to look at the wax figures of emperors and kings, of heroes and murderers of the day. The dead now had that same unreality, which shocks without arousing pity.

I stood in the trench cutting into the earth with my pick. The point stuck, and I heaved and pulled it out with a jerk. With it came a slimy, shapeless bundle, and when I bent down to look I saw that wound round my pick were human entrails. A dead man was buried there.

A—dead—man.

What made me pause then? Why did those three words startle me so? They closed upon my brain like a vice; they choked my throat and chilled my heart. Three words, like any other three words.

A dead man—I tried to thrust the words out of my mind. What was there about them that they should so overwhelm me?

A—dead—man—

And suddenly, like light in darkness, the real truth broke in upon me. The simple fact of Man, which I had forgotten, which had lain deep buried and out of sight; the idea of community, of unity.

A dead man.

Not a dead Frenchman.

Not a dead German.

A dead man.

All these corpses had been men; all these corpses had breathed as I breathed; had had a father, a mother, a woman whom they loved, a piece of land which was theirs, faces which expressed their joys and their sufferings, eyes which had known the light of day and the color of the sky. At that moment of realization I knew that I had been blind because I had wished not to see; it was only then that I realized, at last, that all these dead men, Frenchmen and Germans, were brothers, and I was the brother of them all.

After that I could never pass a dead man without stopping to gaze on his face stripped by death of that earthly patina which masks the living soul. And

I would ask, Who were you? Where was your home? Who is mourning for you now? But I never asked who was to blame. Each had defended his own country; the Germans Germany, the Frenchmen France; they had done their duty.

I was fetching some coffee from the field kitchen when I came across a soldier sitting by the road, a mere boy with the gray uniform hanging loosely about his undeveloped body, as though he were dressed up in his father's clothes. The boy was crying, his face buried in his hands, his nails pressed deep into his palms. Then his arms fell limply to his side, and he sank down in a heap.

"What is it?" I asked.

The boy shuddered and did not look up.

"What is it?" I asked again.

The boy sat there rigidly, the tears welling from his eyes. I put my hand on his shoulder, and with a weary jerk of the head he indicated something behind him.

Lying there was another soldier, another boy. I lifted the cap that covered his face. His blond hair fell in a tangle over his narrow forehead; and his eyes, set in a thin sharp face, were closed. His mouth and chin were no more than a bleeding pulp: the boy was dead.

"He was my friend. We were at the same school, and in the same class. He was a year younger than I; nearly seventeen. I joined up on my own accord, but he couldn't go at first: his mother wouldn't let him. He was her only son. He was ashamed; and we both argued and argued until at last she gave in. We only got to the front a week ago; and now he's dead. What can I write to his mother?"

"Say that he has done his duty," I wanted to say, but I didn't say it. There was a stale taste in my mouth. I seized my coffee-pot and cried: "Don't write anything!" And then: "Stop howling, kid!"

Spring came round again, and in the clearings of the wood grass sprang up from the soldiers' graves. The graves were shallow, too shallow; the rain had washed away the thin covering of earth from one so that two clumsy leather boots showed above the soil in ghastly nakedness.

"Size ten," said a Berlin infantry man who was standing next to me.

In those two boots were two decaying legs; legs which had marched across the battle-fields of France and Russia; legs which had learned the goose-step and had marched on parade past generals, perhaps past the Kaiser himself; legs which had stood to attention at the sergeant's command; legs which had known how to change formation on the march; legs which in war had been more valuable than a head, less valuable than a rifle. Millions of legs were decaying all over Europe, all buried in their boots, as dead kings are buried with their scepters. With my bayonet I broke up the heavy clods of earth, and covered up the boots which had "done their duty."

Behind our line a French aeroplane was brought down in flames. The machine was completely shattered, the pilot burned to a cinder; only his boots of yellow Russian leather came through unscathed. They were immediately appropriated by a corporal from the second battery, and he showed them off to the French girls in the village. *"Commes elles sont chics!"* the girls laughed. "Real French!" laughed the corporal; and he related their history. The girls cast down their eyes, mutely and fearfully.

"Airman *kaput, la France kaput!"* said the corporal.

"Jamais!" one of the girls retorted hotly.

"I and you *amour,"* said the corporal.

I was at the front for thirteen months, and by the end of that time the sharpest perceptions had become dulled, the greatest words mean. The war had become an everyday affair, life in the line a matter of routine; instead of heroes there were only victims; conscripts instead of volunteers; life had become hell, death a bagatelle. We were all of us cogs in a great machine which sometimes rolled forward, nobody knew where, sometimes backwards, nobody knew why. We had lost our enthusiasm, our courage, the very sense of our identity; there was no rhyme or reason in all this slaughter and devastation; pain itself had lost its meaning; the earth was a barren waste.

We used to hack away the copper guiding rings of unexploded shells out of sheer perversity; only the other day one had exploded and blown up two men—but what did that matter?

I applied for a transfer to the Air Force, not from any heroic motive, or for love of adventure, but simply to get away from the mass, from mass-living and mass-dying.

But before my transfer came through I fell ill. Heart and stomach both broke down, and I was sent back to a hospital in Strassburg. In a quiet Franciscan monastery kind and silent monks looked after me. After many weeks I was discharged—unfit for further service.

5. An Attempt to Forget

I began attending lectures at the University of Munich. My enthusiasm was boundless; a fierce curiosity drove me from subject to subject. I listened to lectures on constitutional law with the same eagerness and earnest expectation as I listened to the Wölfflin lectures on Dürer and Holbein. Nothing escaped me; paragraphs and pandects, form and style, all seemed to hold a secret which I was determined to surprise—a meaning, a law. The more I learned the more I thirsted to learn; but truth itself, which was what I sought, remained elusive.

I specially enjoyed Professor Kutscher's course on the history of literature. A neat figure in his captain's uniform, he would stand on the rostrum with the iron cross pinned on his chest, leaning lightly on his crutch. He was a good friend to us moderns, and every week would invite us to a café where Thomas Mann, Karl Henckell, and Max Halbe read to us from their works, and Frank Wedekind in his hard staccato chanted his splendid diabolical ballads. Afterwards we used to wander for hours through the dark streets, bandying the fashionable critical clichés of

92

the moment, praising, condemning, defending. Each of us had a drawer full of manuscripts; each dreamed of fame; each deemed himself specially favored and chosen.

Every time we met a fellow called Weiss had finished a new volume of verse. He wrote twelve poems a day, sometimes even fifteen; rhymed verse in the morning, vers libre in the afternoon and evening. He wrote them in thick notebooks, lyrics in red ink, tragic verse in black. Goethe, he declared, had produced eighty volumes in his lifetime, and he hoped to achieve two hundred and fifty. I, who could only boast of a single slender notebook, regarded this industry with envy and despair.

One day Thomas Mann invited me to his house, and I stuffed my pockets full of manuscripts. During tea I was inwardly much agitated as to when would be the right moment to read him one or two poems. At last I summoned up courage. "Hm," he said when I had finished, "hm." Was that praise or blame? He took the manuscripts from me, and went over them with me line by line—praising this, explaining why that was not good enough. His patience was wonderful, and his advice kind though penetrating. He kept one or two poems and two days later wrote me a long letter; he had been through them again, and had still more advice for the young man who has never forgotten this extraordinary courtesy.

In a bookshop one day I met Rainer Maria Rilke.

"I've written no poetry for years, now," he said gently. "The war has made me dumb."

The war? The word darkened the day. I had not read a newspaper for weeks; I had been trying to forget the war.

I visited the art galleries. I went with the woman I loved to the Bavarian lakes; we went to concerts— Bach, Beethoven, Schubert. In the pulsing of the music I was able to forget the accusation of that man who took three days to die on the wire of no man's land.

Everything was new and blessed: warmth and quiet, books and the words of friends; the solicitude of my landlady, hot baths, bed. "Out there" I had gone for weeks on end without taking off my clothes, sleeping at night on rotting straw or on the cold, wet earth. After a year at the front, I remember, I went on short leave; and on the way home I stayed for twenty-four hours in Berlin. I had booked a room in one of the most comfortable hotels, determined to rest there only for an hour, and then go out and watch the varied life of the streets: cafés, shop windows, women. But when I slid between the cool white sheets I forgot Berlin, and spent the whole twenty-four hours in bed.

Now in Munich in the early spring I used to wander through the English Gardens; snow-drops were showing, and crocuses, and the first violets; the trees were thick with new buds, swollen with the rising sap; behind them glowed the fresh green velvet of distant lawns. Girls sat in front of the Pavilion in their bright frocks; children sang in time to the music of the band, and everywhere was happiness. I breathed peace and sunlight deep into my lungs. I wanted to forget the war.

I could not forget it. For four weeks, for six weeks, all went well; then suddenly it came over me again; soon I was face to face with it at every turn. Standing in front of the altar of Mathias Grünewald I looked past it to the witches' cauldron of the Bois-le-Prêtre and saw my friends there, dead and mangled. I met crippled soldiers in the streets and black-veiled sorrowing women. Oh, there was no escape!

She lay still at my side, and the warm night breeze rustled through the open window.

"You're trembling."

"Please shut the window."

"Is it that singing in the street?"

"It's so cold."

"What is it, my darling?"

"Do they bury the dead in coffins out there?"

"In tent cloth."

"Always?"

"Except in the common graves."

"The thought of that dreadful cold haunts me so that even this little warmth of ours seems swallowed up."

"Come closer to me."

"I love you. My friend has just been killed at Verdun." 95

6. Revolt

On one of the gentle hills of central Germany, among the blue-green fir slopes of Thuringia, stands Burg Lauenstein; and to this castle Eugen Diederichs, the publisher, used to invite scholars, artists, publicists, social reformers and all sorts of young men. At that time of stress, when so many people were all at sea, they would discuss together the problems and tendencies of the day.

I was there with Max Weber, the Heidelberg Sociologist; Max Maurenbrecher who had taken orders but had become the foremost politician and social reformer of the day; the poets Richard Dehmel and Walter von Molo; Bröger, the worker-poet; Kroner the sculptor; and many scholars, including Meinecke, Sombart, Tönnies. The war had driven them all from their study tables; they were all questioning the values of yesterday and today. But the young wanted something more than theorizing. To them the world into which they had been born seemed ripe for annihilation, and they sought for a way out of the dreadful confusion of the times; they sought to make a new order out of chaos; they believed in the

96

absolute, incorruptible mind which should recognize no master but the truth. But these men whom they honored as standard-bearers of the intellect were no Biblical prophets to condemn the familiar ways and reveal the new; they were not ready to brave the rage of kings and tyrants, nor were they rebels and constructors; they took shelter behind glittering and romantic phrases. There were those who held that the moment had come for the new, the unique, German spirit, founded on a religion, that should arise and save the world. Others pinned their faith to the foundation of a German church, and had drawn up plans for a great temple which was to stand on the highest mountain in Germany for all to see, a meeting place for the faithful. Max Maurenbrecher declared that the curse of the age was the democratic individualism of Western Europe; and that Germany, the instrument of God, having destroyed this by means of the war ought now to fulfill her mission of creating a new State of Europe, a State which should be an earthly symbol of the Absolute.

But it was to Max Weber that most of the youth of the day turned, profoundly attracted by his intellectual honesty. He loathed political romanticism, and attacked Maurenbrecher bitterly and with him all those German scholars whose fine-spun theories were utterly out of touch with reality. What is the use, he would say, of finding one's own soul when the nation itself gropes in outer darkness? The German State was an autocracy, and the people had had no voice in

97

its foundation. The Prussian Class-franchise must go, so must bureaucratic rule; we must have Parliamentary government, and a democratic control. But all these questions could only be dealt with when we saw how the war ended.

There were others there who sought to drug themselves with medieval mysteries which were to re-awaken community-feeling. Poets chanted dithyrambs, and the poet Falke made his daughters dance in the moonlight before the ivy-covered walls of the castle. The quality of their dancing was of no account; they believed that the spirit of God hovered over the dancers. Through dim, tapestried chambers where ancient worm-eaten furniture loomed ghost-like in the dark, they walked in the twilight feeling like medieval knights, missionaries of the Holy Ghost.

And so it went on, talk, endless talk, while the battlefields of Europe shuddered beneath the blows of war. We waited, we still waited, for these men to speak the word of deliverance; in vain. Were they deaf and dumb and blind? Was it because they themselves had never lain in a dugout, never heard the despairing cries of the dying, the dumb accusation of a devastated wood; never looked into the desperate eyes of a hunted refugee?

I was young and immature, and all these men were far wiser, maturer, more experienced than I, so that to speak before them seemed presumptuous. But I had to speak. And I cried: "Show us the way; we sit here wasting day after day, when every minute counts. We have waited long enough!" But they were all silent. The dancers went on dancing and the visionaries building their new church, their mystic temple, with resounding phrases.

There remained only two men: these were Richard Dehmel and Max Weber, whose fighting temperament had often shown itself in our evening conversations. With words which endangered life and freedom Max Weber laid bare the Reich and exposed its evils. The greatest evil seemed to him the Kaiser, and he declared that when the war was over he would publicly insult that conceited dilettante until he was forced to take action against him, and then the responsible statesmen, Bülow, Bethmann-Hollweg, Tirpitz, would be compelled to give evidence under oath. Brave words, but they made it clear what separated us from him. We were concerned with more than the sins of the Kaiser, with more than reforming the franchise. We wanted to create a whole new world, believing that to change the existing order would be also to change the hearts of men.

The poet Dehmel had known the war, for he had joined up in 1914, although he was fifty, and had come home weary and troubled. Once when we walked together through the Thuringian forest he encouraged me to recite some of my poems to him. "Don't think about us back-numbers," he said. "Go your own way, even though the world persecutes you and obstructs you. That poem of yours which

99

ends: I died / Was reborn / Died / Was reborn / I was my own mother—that's all that matters. Once in his life every man must cast adrift from everything, even from his mother; he must become his own mother."

I left Lauenstein and went to Heidelberg for the winter term. Everyone was studying economics, not knowing what else to do with themselves. It was at once a need and a fashion. In every stratum of German society it was the thing to do to take a doctor's degree; and even if you were not a doctor the worthless title was conferred on you by every landlady and innkeeper, every waiter and prostitute. Heidelberg had the reputation of being a doctor factory. Questions set by the good-humored old Professor Gothein for the last several decades are edited for cramming and sold with answers.

He instructed me for my thesis on "Pig-breeding in East Prussia."

Heidelberg in wartime had little in common with the pretty-pretty romanticism of the Old Heidelberg films. The majority of the students were sick men and cripples back from the war.

The innkeepers bewailed the passing of the days when the students' corps used to march down the streets in their gay-colored caps and sashes, and when good beer flowed like water. The landladies regarded the women students with cold dislike for the way they went through their bills every month and cross-examined every pfennig.

I had been bitterly disappointed by my stay at Lauenstein. There had been nothing but words, words, words.

But they had said nothing. Which of them at last would give the word? The author of *The Weavers* perhaps, Gerhart Hauptmann? He had written a play for the centenary of the Battle of Leipzig in which he condemned war and exalted peace, and which had called down the wrath of the Hohenzollerns on his head. In 1914, like many other German authors, he had been swept off his feet by the war-fever; he turned out battle hymns and soldiers' songs. But now, after all these murderous years, he must have found himself again. I wrote to him:

"You must not remain silent any longer. It is your duty to speak. We, the young men, are awaiting the word of a spiritual leader in whom we can believe. You made a mistake—who does not?—but now it is for you, the poet of suffering humanity, to acknowledge your mistake. Your words are more powerful than the commands of kings; they would be a trumpet call to peace, and all the youth of Europe would rise up in response."

No answer came from Gerhart Hauptmann.

The war continued as before. Every day brought news of fresh engagements, further casualties. Every handbreadth of land lost or won meant hecatombs of dead. The end seemed as far away as ever.

At Heidelberg I was invited out a good deal. Everybody wanted to discuss the day's problems. We drank German war-tea made of dried lime-blossoms and ate German war-biscuits made of clay and potato flour. In the course of time I made some new friends: young people who realized that the "great time" was a time of misery, who condemned war with its insensate sacrifice of life, whose only desire was to isolate the few grains of truth in the vast desert of lies. Yet even they shrank from the actions which were the logical outcome of their words. They would go home after an evening's sincere and excited argument; they would return to their badly heated, hideously furnished rooms in the tranquil faith that something would happen sooner or later. I used to listen to their discussions and think of Lauenstein with its endless flood of words, its cowardliness and inertia.

Didn't we swear to our friends out there on the field of death, crouched together below the parapet or huddled together in the dugout, in shattered woods and villages, under the hail of shrapnel, and beneath the light of the stars—didn't we swear then by all that was most sacred that one good thing must come out of the war—an uprising of youth? Europe must be rebuilt, its foundations laid anew. Our fathers had betrayed us, and the young who had known war, hard and unsentimental, would begin the business of spring-cleaning. If we had not the right to, who had?

And remembering this in the security of Heidelberg I burst out: "All these vague complaints are simply futile! There is only one way for us. We must revolt!"

There was silence after I spoke. Some timid souls took up their coats and left; the others banded themselves together for rebellion. We called ourselves the "Young Germans' Cultural and Political Union"; we were to fight for the peaceful solution of social problems and anomalies and for the elimination of poverty; for we thought that if poverty disappeared the urge to seize foreign land and money, to subjugate foreign peoples and subdue foreign States, would automatically disappear also. Only the poor, we declared, can be misled; if you have enough to eat yourself you do not covet your neighbor's bread; it seemed evident that war and poverty were fatally complementary. Nobody had any idea of the way to eliminate poverty, nobody knew how to solve social problems peacefully; all we knew was that it had to be done.

We were soon attacked by the German Fatherland Party, who denounced us as betrayers of our land, as criminal pacifists. We answered:

"You misuse the word Fatherland. Your private interests are not the interests of the people. We know that no foreign power can crush our culture, but we repudiate any attempt to force our own culture upon another nation. Our goal is not aggrandizement, but cultural enrichment; it is spiritual not material development.

"We want to rouse the apathetic and indifferent into

103

action, and we heartily respect those students in other countries who have already begun to protest against the unthinkable stupidity and horror of the war."

This answer was published in the papers, and as a result of it several well-known people wrote us encouraging letters, among them Foerster and Einstein. But these were a thousand times outnumbered by the abusive and threatening letters which came by every post.

The reactionary newspapers urged the authorities to take action against us, and democratic University dons denounced us as pacifists. The *Berliner Tageblatt* printed our answer to these attacks.

"The epithets 'dishonorable' and 'unpatriotic' have always been applied to unpopular opinions. Is it 'unpatriotic' to strive for the peaceful union of free and independent nations? Is that extenuating the evils of any particular government? Is that 'demanding Peace at any price'? If so, our German language has lost its meaning.

"The fact that there are relatively few of us in no way invalidates our argument. Our idea of politics is that each one of us must assume responsibility for the destiny of the people; whoever does not believe this can have no real conscience. There is only one morality which is worth anything to mankind. Those of us who have actually experienced war feel themselves doubly bound to hold to the path they have chosen. We know that only so are we truly helping our brothers out there. We love Germany, perhaps in our own way; we demand much from it—but much also from ourselves."

Then the High Command launched its attack, warning the youth of Germany against sedition, and the military authorities began to act.

All the Austrian students belonging to our League were ordered to leave Germany within twenty-four hours. All the male members had to report to the District Commandant. Even those who had been pronounced unfit for active service were suddenly declared A 1 and sent to barracks.

The day this persecution began in earnest I was in a hospital, ill with a fever. A girl came to tell me that they were already searching for me in my rooms.

"You will have to get away from here at once," she said, "or you'll be arrested!"

A little later I sat shivering and feverish in the Berlin train. Next day I went to the Reichstag and gave the alarm to the Democratic and Socialist Deputies. Our League was still banned and so too were all the other little groups which had been formed at other Universities. But our society was a portent. We had started to revolt against war. We believed that our voices would be heard the other side of no man's land and that the youth of every country would join us in our fight against those whom we accused as the originators of the war: our fathers!

The evening before my flight from Heidelberg a letter came from Gustav Landauer, whose *Summons to Socialism* had so decisively moved me. I answered him thus:

"It is not simply necessity which has driven me to do what I am doing, not only pain in face of hideous everyday happenings, not only indignation at the political and economic system; these have all counted, of course, but there is more behind it than that.

"I am not a mystic concerned only with relations between myself and God to the exclusion of the rest of humanity. I pity those who can think only of their own personal little troubles. I pity those whose hysterical enthusiasm for the movement demands futurist cabarets and revolution with equal emphasis. No, I am determined to embrace life in all its manifestations. For all that, I believe that dead wood must be cut out. No one has a right to life who has nothing to give. I demand of those who would go with us not merely devotion to the needs of spirit alone, or of mind, or of body, but devotion to man in all his needs.

"I am not dreaming of a band of community creators; for the creative spirit manifests itself in its purest form in the work of individuals; but community feeling is encouraging and stimulating to creation. I know the ideas I am fighting against, and I imagine that I also know what ideas must supersede them; but I still cannot visualize with any clearness the exterior forms that these new ideas must take.

"I am conscious of an inner peace which is freedom, which gives me freedom. I know that my mind is far from peaceful, that I can still fight bitterly and violently against dirt and ignorance; but yet this sense of inner peace remains."

7. Strike

One day I found on my table a parcel of books containing among other things the memoirs of Lichnowsky, Muhlon, and Beerfeld.

The World War had turned me into an opponent of war. I had already realized that it had been a catastrophe for Europe, a plague on humanity, the crime of our century. Thoughts as to who was responsible for it had never entered my head. Now I read in these books that the Imperial Government had betrayed the nation, that it was as much to blame as anybody else for the war, as much to blame for its continuance. It isn't true, I said over and over again. It isn't true. But here were men who could prove their accusations. The Government had done nothing to prevent the Austrian monarchy making war on Serbia; the Government had violated the neutrality of Belgium, although in so doing it broke its pledge and knew that England would declare war the moment Belgium was invaded. In this war the German people was not defending itself; in this war I was not defending my country; no, German steel magnates had coveted the Belgian mines, were deter-

107

mined to seize Longwy and Briey for themselves. And now the aims of the pan-German Imperialists were delaying peace. We had been betrayed. Our efforts had been in vain. In the light of this revelation my world crashed to pieces before my eyes. I had been as credulous as everyone else in Germany, as credulous as the nameless masses.

When I turned out the light that night I could find no sleep. The day came round once more, but the day brought no light; I felt that the land I loved had been betrayed and sold. It was for us to overthrow these betrayers; there was guilt also in France, in Russia, in England, in Italy; but we were Germans, and must put our own house in order first.

But the question of war-guilt involved more than individuals; the rulers themselves were entangled in a vast mesh of vested interests, of moral concepts and established social values. They sought to build the power and honor and freedom of their people upon the impotence and misery and oppression of other peoples. But no people is truly free unless its neighbors also are free. The politicians had deceived themselves just as they had deceived the people. They called their interests ideals, and for these ideals—for gold, land, mines, oil, for dead things—for such ideals men must die and hunger and despair. The question of war-guilt pales before the guilt of capitalism.

Until then the workers' movement and its aim had been strange to me. At school we had been taught that the Socialists were out to destroy the State, and that their leaders were blackguards with a sharp eye for their own interests. But now, for the first time, I came to know a workers' leader, Kurt Eisner.

Eisner came for a short visit to Berlin, and some friends took me to see him. Even in the early days of the war he had made himself known as its opponent, and the military authorities had persecuted and silenced him, while to his own party he was a burden and a nuisance. But he was not to be deterred, and he persisted in his campaign against war. When, later on, a little group broke away from the main Social Democratic party and called itself the "Independents," he joined them and continued his activities in Munich. Thus, among the workers, the movement against the Kaiser's war policy grew steadily. They had no faith in the leaders who voted more and more money for the war; they put their faith in Liebknecht, the outlaw, the jailbird, the visionary.

A few days later I found myself in Munich, attending Eisner's meetings with workers, women and young people, all seeking the way to achieve peace and rescue the people. At these meetings I saw worker personalities whom I had never met before; men of keen understanding, of deep insight into social problems, of profound experience of life, of sober intellect, of iron will—Socialists who without considering the interests of the day worked single-mindedly for the things in which they believed.

Then, one day, ten thousand munition workers

came out on strike at Kiel, and demanded "peace without annexations or indemnities," and self-determination for the people. What would Munich do? The Social Democrats didn't want to strike, and Eisner and the Independents were too weak to bring it off alone; but in spite of that the strike came. The first to come out were the Krupp workers, most of them North Germans. They were impervious to all threats. "Your food rations will be reduced; you will be conscripted and sent to the front." But they feared neither privation nor death. They were not fighting for an increase in wages; their fight had nothing to do with their own needs, for they were a privileged body, exempt from active service; they were fighting for their brothers at the front.

A strike committee was formed, of which Eisner was a member. I attended the strikers' meetings; I wanted to help, to do anything that I could. I distributed among the women some of my verses and the cripple and hospital scenes from my play, *Die Wandlung*, because I believed that these verses, born of the horror of war, might touch them and strike home.

At last I was given a job to do; I was to address the women workers of a big factory, to persuade them to join the strikers. The gatekeeper refused me admission to the great courtyard, but some workers came to my aid, and soon all the women were assembled there. They laid down tools, and we all went together to the meeting.

There was some anxiety, for Eisner, who was to speak, had not arrived; neither had the rest of the strike committee. After an hour of fruitless waiting we learned that they had all been arrested the night before.

Among the prisoners was Frau Sonja Lerch, the wife of a university don. Her husband had disowned her on the first day of the strike, but she loved him and could not leave him. The evening before her arrest she came to see me, unhappy and distraught. I told her she could stay the night in my room, and warned her not to go back to her husband's house, for the police would be sure to look for her there. But she was deaf to my entreaties. "I must see him once more; just once more," she repeated over and over again, like a child clamoring for the broken bits of a dearly loved doll. She went, and the police came for her at three o'clock in the morning, and took her to Stadelheim prison. There she cried aloud night and day, and her cries echoed through the cells and the corridors and froze the blood of prisoners and warders alike. On the fourth day they found her dead. She had hanged herself.

But a mass movement which believes in its goal is not to be stemmed by the arrest of its leaders. The deciding element is faith; only when faith begins to sicken, to weaken and to die can the opposing power smash the unity of the movement, break it into helpless, vacillating fragments. But these workers had faith, and they replied to the news of their leaders' arrest by electing a delegation to wait on the President of Police and demand their release. The three thousand assembled strikers were to accompany the delegation to police headquarters, and if they did not reappear in an hour a second delegation was to follow them. The meeting did not break up, and the strike continued with undiminished strength.

The first delegation was chosen, and the chairman asked for volunteers for the second delegation. Three shouted out their names, among them a soldier; but only two mounted the platform; at the last moment the soldier drew back. Calls for a third volunteer were in vain; nobody answered. Then I gave my name, and the chairman asked me to say a few words; and thus for the first time I addressed a mass meeting. For the first few sentences I stuttered, awkward and embarrassed; but suddenly I got into my stride and spoke easily and effortlessly without knowing where the power of my speaking came from.

Outside in the street the strikers formed into a procession, and we marched to police headquarters. On the way we passed the Life Guards barracks; the windows were jammed with men back from the front who waved at us encouragingly.

As we approached the Wittelsbach Palace, the barrack gates opened and a squad of young recruits, led by a lieutenant, marched rapidly past our procession, halted just in front of the Palace, deployed and stood like a living wall barring the street. Pale and excited, the lieutenant drew his revolver and ordered the seventeen-year-old country lads—none of them had ever seen the front—to load and make ready. Our procession came to a sudden halt. Should we break through the cordon? Should we fight? Next moment the first shot of our civil war rang out. They had weapons; we had none. Our leaders conferred together indecisively. An old worker shouted: "We want our rights, we don't want bloodshed."

The procession turned down a side-street; but that street also was barricaded. We checked once more. The first delegation started off, and the police allowed them through. The door opened to their summons, and they disappeared inside.

We waited. An hour went by; still they did not come out. Then we of the second delegation set out. The police made a way for us, and we went inside. Before we could say anything the President of Police turned to one of us whom he appeared to recognize.

"Weren't you in my company at the front?"

The man mechanically clicked his heels. "Yes, sir."

"And now you've turned traitor?"

"We are not traitors," I said. "We are trying to save Germany, not betray her."

"I don't know who you are," said the President.

"What does that matter? I'm speaking for others, not for myself; for thousands of others who demand the release of their arrested leaders."

"Stand to attention"—the President wanted to say;

he glared at me, but his glance wavered and became uncertain; instead of a command came the familiar words:

"I have no authority to release them."

We returned to our procession. We felt we must let people know the truth. The papers were maligning the strikers, and we ought to issue a leaflet of our own, and that at once.

We went to the house of a Social Democrat, a town councilor who had no sympathy with the strikers, but whose son was on our side. I had scarcely drafted our appeal before the front door bell rang, and our friend's sister called out "Police!" We had carelessly failed to notice that the police had been following us to the house. I rolled the paper up into a ball, and stuffed it into the stove which was not alight. But the police weren't after us; they arrested the father and took him away. We stared dazedly at each other, rescued the paper ball, smoothed it out and finished writing. Then we took the fair copy to a printer, and knew that in a few hours thousands of copies would be distributed in the streets of Munich. Then, like a fool, instead of burning the rough draft, I stuffed it into my coat pocket.

Next day fifty thousand workers assembled in the Theresienwiese. The police could only look on helplessly as they marched past, could only listen helplessly to our speeches. They dared not attack or arrest the speakers.

The strike went on for days until the Social Democrats took over the leadership; they had promised the War Ministry to break the strike, and this was the means they chose to fulfill their promise. A delegation had previously been chosen to put before the Minister "with all seriousness and with all due emphasis" the demands of the strikers. Auer, the Social Democratic leader, managed to soothe the discontented workers; he guaranteed the fulfillment of their demands and undertook to lead the delegation to the War Minister and to see that nobody who had taken part in the strike should be dismissed or punished. In the morning the strikers gathered for a final demonstration in the Theresienwiese, passed in procession through the city, and dispersed in the Karlsplatz.

At midday I was having lunch in my rooms when the maid announced two gentlemen who wished to see me.

"What can I do for you?" I asked.

"Hands up!" they shouted, and I found myself looking down the barrel of a revolver.

I was under arrest. My captors clicked handcuffs on my wrists and took me first to the police station, then to the barracks where I had to sit in a little wooden cubicle partitioned off from the guard room.

In the guard room the men behaved as though I were non-existent, joked and ate and played cards. I felt as insubstantial as air.

I called out to a passing soldier; but he ignored me. The guard had been forbidden to speak to me.

After a time I was taken to the bathroom, and an N.C.O. threw a dirty uniform at me.

"Put that on!"

I refused. "I've been invalided out."

"Well, you've been called up again. Put that on!"

"You can't conscript me without a medical examination!"

So then they dressed me forcibly. The military uniform worked a transformation in me; my "pride" was wounded, for they had given me a private's uniform.

"Where are the stripes?" I said. "I'm an N.C.O."

Later I was taken to be questioned. For hours they cross-examined me. They firmly believed that Germany was honey-combed with secret societies, and the truer my answers the more incredible they seemed. My examiner tried to twist the simplest statements; my most spontaneous answers were made out to be calculated; everything that had happened accidentally he persisted in regarding as having been carefully planned. He was convinced that somewhere there was an all-powerful central office directing the workers' movements. He was entirely incapable of grasping the true motive of the strike; to him the people were simply a body without a head, an unstable mass who only fought when spurred on and misled by agitators. And when he solemnly asked me who had provided the immense sum necessary, as he thought, to finance the strike, I burst out laughing;

116

for we ourselves had all spent our last pfennigs on paper for our leaflets.

"You'll soon laugh on the wrong side of your face!" he said, as he left the room. At the door he turned and called "Sentry!"

A soldier came into the room.

"You are responsible for the prisoner."

The door slammed behind him.

The door opened again after a moment, and an officer entered and busied himself about the room, but I could see he was looking at me closely.

"Are they giving you a bad time?"

"Only this examination."

"I was in the next room, and heard everything. Do you smoke?" He offered me a cigarette. Then he came closer and his voice was low and scornful:

"Stand up to him. Cross-examining isn't everybody's game, and it's not his. You've got to be born to it."

He left me staring after him in astonishment.

In due course my examiner came back with a leather case under his arm. He opened it, searched for a moment, and produced a copy of our leaflet.

"Do you know this?"

"No."

"You don't, don't you? Are you quite sure?"

Then he looked in his case again, and produced a crumpled sheet of paper—the rough draft.

"Do you still deny it?"

I said nothing.

"We cut open your coat. There was a hole in the pocket, and this was in the lining. Take him away!"

I was taken through the streets of Munich by an N.C.O. and two privates with fixed bayonets. The people stood and stared, and children ran after us.

"Murderer!" one of them cried.

Then the gates of the military prison in the Leonrodstrasse closed behind me.

8. The Military Prison

The prison on the Leonrodstrasse was one of the oldest in Munich. The offices and the corridors had electric light, but the cells no lighting at all; and in those gloomy winter days nightfall for the prisoners came at three o'clock in the afternoon and lasted until late the next morning. We could read for only a few hours in the middle of the day.

I made good use of my time there. I read Marx, Engels, Lassalle, Bakunin, Mehring, Luxemburg, the Webbs. It had been more by accident than by reasoned intention that I had allied myself with the strikers, for what had drawn me to them was their struggle to end the war. But in my prison cell I discovered the meaning of Socialism, and for the first time I saw clearly the true structure of society today, the conditions that make war inevitable, the terrible perversity of the law that allows the masses to go hungry while a few grow rich, the true relationship between labor and capital, the historical significance of the working class.

I found myself thinking again of Stanislaus, my childhood friend, of his hatred of the rich, and of my mother's answer when I asked her why some people were so poor: "Because it's God's will." I saw that there was food enough to spare for every living being, that the human mind had found ways and means of conquering nature, of literally turning stone into gold and gold into bread. Yet men were still dying of starvation, while good wheat was being dumped into the sea; there were still vast empty palaces while outside their gates wandered those who had no home; there were still men who squandered fortunes on a toy while children grew up stunted and deformed for lack of light. And more even than this, I saw that the things of the mind were a closed book to the poor, and that the noblest powers of humanity were broken, shattered, sacrificed without end on the altars of false gods. The people were ruled by blindness and unreason, and bore their tyranny because they distrusted reason; reason which can create order out of chaos and reintegrate confusion. Since man himself grows organically he calls his idols, Industry and the State, organic growth too, and thus silences the voice of conscience, for is he not helpless in face of the unthinkable, the irresistible power of a world which offers death as final and ineluctable reward? The fear of death strikes deep and gnaws ever at his consciousness. He prizes freedom, and yet fears it; he would rather bend to the yoke and forge his own fetters than stand free with the responsibilities of freedom.

Every day I was allowed half an hour's exercise round and round the prison yard. With spring came the first buds on the little shrubs; poor, stunted little shrubs they were, but to me they were like blazing rhododendrons. Verses used to come to me during this daily exercise—the *Songs of Prison* and the closing scenes of *Die Wandlung*.

The cells were filthy and infested with lice. The rough blankets were used by dozens of prisoners, one after another, before they were changed. Our food consisted of war-bread mixed with clay, turnip soup, turnip jam, turnip tops, and, on Sundays, barley soup with a minute shred of meat in it. We were always hungry.

We were prisoners. But we were also soldiers, and we were forbidden to take our shoes off all day, to undo more than one button of our uniform jackets. Every offense against regulations was severely punished. The place was overflowing with deserters, and to make room for new prisoners they were given the option of being sent back to the front or transferred to a civil prison. In the old days it had been considered an honor to serve with the forces, but now it was offered as an alternative to prison.

The warders were *Landwehr* men who had been invalided out, and they were fairly easy to get on with; but the N.C.O.s in the office had never been anywhere near the front and treated us with cynical brutality. I once saw one of them, a mean, undersized little rat, box the ears of a great, brawny fellow until he burst into tears. And many of the prisoners chose death rather than endure the hell of their days, opening their arteries with splinters, tearing their bed-coverings into strips to make a noose for their necks, jumping from the banisters onto the stone floor below. I shall never forget the shrill, animal cry that startled me out of my sleep one morning and made me cry out myself with a strange and alien voice.

The warders were kind to me; they would come and talk to me in my cell, and ask if the *ramp* would ever come to an end, and tell me about their wives and children, and the lack of food everywhere. But when I told them that only their own efforts could shorten the war, they would shrug their shoulders and repeat the old cowardly phrase:

"Well, of course, if everybody else would do the same."

The other strike-leaders had all been arrested, but I saw nothing of them; we were strictly isolated from one another. Apparently the authorities had not dared publish the fact that we had been arrested for the part we played in the strike. The *Münchener Post*, the Social Democratic paper, had said that we were imprisoned for desertion. Nor was I allowed to receive visitors, not even my lawyer. The only way to indicate my resistance was to go on a hunger-strike.

Day after day I was taken up for reëxamination, until finally the clerk read over to me a statement which I refused to sign, protesting that it was full of distortions and misrepresentations. Schuler, the military lawyer, glared at me and ordered me to stand to attention.

"I command you to sign this statement."

I did not move.

"You'll get dark cells and bread and water if you don't."

Still I said nothing.

Next day I was again recalled and ordered to sign.

"I will not," I said; and then, driven by hunger, fever, and uncontrollable rage, I flung myself at him.

"You blackguard!" I cried, and then realized what a hopeless position I was in.

The man shrank back and smiled wryly.

"Good. If you won't sign I'll have to sign it myself."

One morning I woke with a sore throat and limbs as heavy as lead; when I tried to get up I collapsed. At midday the doctor came, a Jew, who examined me, told me that all pacifists should be stood against a wall and shot, prescribed aspirin, and refused to allow me a second blanket. All that night I lay in a raging fever, and nobody came near me. But next day another doctor came, and when he had got the official with him out of the cell on some pretext or other he bent over my bed and said:

"I loathe the war just as much as you. I'll do whatever I can for you. For the moment I'll have you taken to the sick-room, and later I'll declare you unfit for prison."

It must be a dream, I thought; I must be delirious.

The official returning almost at once, the doctor said sharply, as though I were a malingerer: "You'll be sent to the sick-room!"

They took me there that same afternoon, and I was admitted by a fanatically patriotic Jewish N.C.O., who told me to thank my lucky stars that the doctor had taken up my case, and that Germany had a right to Belgium, and to Calais too, for if Germany didn't take it England would.

The prison sick-room was intended for two; but there were six of us—deserters, thieves, murderers, and "traitors." There were beds for two; the other four lay on straw mattresses on the floor. The window was bolted and barred and the air was pestilential: one chamber-pot served all six of us and was emptied only twice a day, at half past six in the morning and at five in, the afternoon. The fellow next to me suffered agonies with a disease of the bladder, and his sodden bed stank like a sewer. He was next to the door, and when the food was handed in through the hatch he would seize the bowl with hands cracked like a washerwoman's. I could not touch the food; the very sight of it made me retch.

The Head of the Medical Staff made his ceremonial visit the next day, attended by the Staff doctor, the assistant Staff doctor, and the second assistant Staff doctor. A book of Werfel's poems, which I had brought with me from the prison, was lying on my bed; the great man picked it up, opened it and read at random:

"Schöpfe Du, trage Du, halte
Tausend Gewässer des Lächelns in Deiner Hand!
Lächeln, selige Feuchte ist ausgespannt
All übers Antlitz!"

"Anyone who reads such bilge can only expect to finish up in prison," he announced and stared expectantly at his suite. The Staff doctor obligingly bowed and laughed, the assistant Staff doctor clicked his heels, the second assistant Staff doctor sprang to attention and bowed deeply.

That concluded the inspection.

I was soon longing for the quiet of my own dirty, lousy cell; it seemed a paradise compared with this hell. After three days of it I insisted that I had recovered, and when I found myself once more in my cell I wept for joy.

The barred window divided the eternal gray of the winter sky into little gloomy squares. If I pulled myself up to the sill I could see on the other side of the courtyard the white court-martial house, where the uniformed curtailers of the rights of man measured out gray prison years. The ground-floor window had friendly white curtains. The porter lived there. And once, at one of the windows two hands parted the curtains and a girl looked out curiously across the courtyard. Our eyes met, and her head disappeared, but the gentle agitation of the curtains betrayed her presence.

The next day at the same time I was again at my grating, and the girl was again at her window; every day at the same hour the friendly ritual was repeated. When the sentries approached and danger threatened she waved to me. She invented a language of expressive gestures; her smiles and glances were the vowels, her hands and shoulders the consonants.

Then one evening the bolt clashed back in the door of my cell, and the warder called me by name.

"Am I to be taken to another prison?" I asked.

"Out you get!" he snapped.

I followed him along the corridor and into his office.

And there, under the warm gas light, was the girl of the window, leaning on the table. I stared at her uncomprehendingly; a wave of color swept her cheeks and she lowered her eyes in confusion.

I was bewildered and apprehensive.

Apparently the porter's daughter was a friend of this warder, and knew, as everybody in the neighborhood knew, that the military prison was being used for political prisoners—romantic adventurers, twentieth century Robin Hoods who robbed the rich to help the poor, fools who preached peace when the nations were at war and when even the priests

126

had declared that God with his angel hosts watched over our army; the sort of people, in short, one reads about in the newspapers—dangerous people, interesting people.

And so this girl had determined to see one of these fascinating creatures for herself. When she asked her lover, however, to smuggle her secretly into the prison he simply laughed at her. But the next evening, when he climbed up to her room as usual, he found the shutters of the window barred; there was no answer when he knocked. Raging inwardly, he had to give it up, for he could already hear voices in her parents' bedroom.

"Why didn't you let me in last night, Marie?" he asked next day.

"Because I didn't want to."

"Can I come tonight?"

"Yes, if you show me one of those poor men."

He offered no more resistance. On the following Sunday he was on duty, with nobody else in the office. He bribed the military guard with cigarettes. And thus it was that I found myself face to face with my girl.

"Well, there is your man," said the warder. "And now I hope you're satisfied."

He sat down at the table, took out a mouth organ from his pocket and began to play it, up and down, up and down.

"If you're going to play, we may as well dance," I said.

"None of your lip!" he said.

"Go on playing," said the girl.

The warder thought of the barred bedroom window, gave a wry smile, and started a waltz.

"May I have the honor?"

"Thank you," said the girl. And we danced round the table to the music of the warder's mouth organ; when we came to the wall where the chains and fetters and handcuffs were hanging I kicked out at them, and we danced on to the accompaniment of their metallic clashing.

Suddenly the music broke off; the warder turned and listened intently.

"Aren't you going to play any more?" the girl asked threateningly.

"Shut up, you silly fool! The boss is coming. This'll cost me my job! Into your cell, you!" And turning to the girl: "You too!"

He pushed me out of the room, and I ran back to my cell, the girl following. The moment the door closed behind us she fell into my arms and we kissed. But the warder was soon with us again.

"False alarm. Come on out of there! That'll do for today."

I had seen nothing of my friend the doctor for some time, but he had not forgotten his promise. One day I was taken to him, and he examined me with a great show of truculence. But a few days later I was released as unfit for further imprisonment, and attached to a reserve battalion at Neu-Ulm.

I wandered down the avenue of blossoming chestnuts that fine spring evening, free, alone. I was happy, but my heart was heavy.

9. The Lunatic Asylum

The rush to enlist was a thing of the past; nobody joined up voluntarily now. The young recruits, children almost, were lashed into some sort of enthusiasm by patriotic schoolmasters; they were taught that Germany had a right to Belgium, to the Baltic Provinces, to more colonies. But they were not impressed by the phrases of their well-nourished lecturers; what impressed them were the rumors that were passing from mouth to mouth, rumors that whole regiments had mutinied at the front, that Austria would soon drop out of the war, that women had been looting grocers' shops and bakers' shops up and down the country. Men were already refusing to be sent up to the line, and the officers were reduced to patient persuasion in order to get them to go. Punishment held no terrors for them. One of them cried out as he was arrested: "Better starve in prison than rot out there!" The men at the front had had enough.

Germany was hungry. Eminent scientists proved that clay had the same food value as flour, that saccharine-sweetened jam was healthier than butter, that dried potato tops were better for the nerves than tobacco and tasted just as good. But the pronouncements of scientists were of little avail to the stomach, which reacted to their nonsense in its own way: people collapsed, fell sick, grew desperate.

There is a German proverb which says: "Hunger is a good cook." But one evening when I saw some Russian prisoners in front of the Neu-Ulm barracks I shuddered at sight of this cook: they threw themselves on the refuse-bins, full of potato peelings and scraps, moldy bread and bones; they dug their hands into the festering stinking heaps and crammed their mouths full.

Whenever we went outside the barracks we had to pass through a crowd of ragged, begging children whose eyes lit up at the sight of a crust of bread.

One Sunday I went in secret to Gustav Landauer at Krumbach. I couldn't understand why, at a time when everybody was waiting for the voice of truth, this ardent revolutionary kept silent. But when I put the question to him he said: "All my life I have worked for the downfall of this social system, this society founded on lies and betrayals, on the beggaring and suppression of human beings; and I know now that this downfall is imminent—perhaps tomorrow, perhaps in a year's time. And I have the right to reserve my strength until that moment. When the hour strikes I shall be there and ready."

I spent the night in the Krumbacher *Gasthaus*, and in the morning, glancing through the visitors' book, I saw that by a strange coincidence my Munich ex-

131

aminer was spending his holiday there. I knew that if he ran into me my re-arrest would be inevitable. I must get away at once. It was dangerous to go by train from Krumbach, so Landauer and I started off for the next station, through private gardens, over fences, across fields. I reached Neu-Ulm safely in the nick of time. The Sergeant-Major had been looking for me. "You're to get ready for a journey," he said. "There's orders come through for you to report at the psychological clinic in Munich."

Apparently my mother had been unable to imagine how her son had come to be accused of treason. The accusation seemed dreadful to her, and no less dreadful the threatened punishment. She could not understand how the son of a bourgeois household could join the workers in their struggle. He must be ill, she had thought; she must help him. So she went to the family doctor, who gave her a certificate which she sent to the Court; hence this psychological examination.

At the clinic I was received by a charming girl who asked me when and where I was born and whether I was single—although she had all my papers in her hand. She smiled kindly at me and her eyes were soft and brown.

"Will you please give me your knife?" she said.

"I haven't one."

"Your money, your handkerchief, and whatever else you have in your pockets."

I stared at her dazedly.

"And now will you come this way?"

A door opened, and a huge warder took charge of me.

"First thing for us is a bath," he said.

"For us?"

He pushed me into a tiled room with three baths, two of them already occupied. One of the occupants was crying aloud in a piercing voice, the other was singing an endless croaking la-lala-la, la-lala-la.

"Off with your clothes!"

"But I've already had one bath today."

The warder stared indifferently over my head.

"I'm not saying you haven't. Take off your clothes."

He doesn't believe me, I thought. He won't believe anything I say. Everything I say he'll take for a lunatic's fancy. Perhaps he thinks that my particular fad is pretending to have a bath every morning. I'm in the hands of a man who is deaf and blind. I must get out. At once. I must get back to the barracks. Anywhere, anyhow. Even to prison. Anywhere but here. I must get out. I'll shout and rave at them. No, that would be fatal; that would finish me. What can I do to convince him? He'll never believe what I say. Never. I looked at the door. A push; a jump; and I would be out.

"There's no handle on that door, nor on the one in the corridor," the warder said.

I undressed and stayed in that place an hour with the man who shrieked and the man who sang, then I got out and put on the trousers that had been laid out for me, and the uniform smock, and followed the warder into a large room where twenty or thirty "unquiet" lunatics were lying. I too was put to bed. I myself began to doubt my senses.

A young man with a short thin neck surmounted by a swollen pumpkin instead of a head was swaying to and fro. He rose from his bed, shambled over to me and solemnly bowed three times. Then he went back to his bed. Every quarter of an hour he repeated the ceremony.

After two days I was referred to the ward for melancholics, and it was not long before I was aching to be back among my singing, shouting, gesticulating friends. In this place thirty pairs of devastated eyes stared in silent emptiness from thirty beds into the graves of their own souls. My neighbor, an old man, laboriously got out of his bed when he saw me, and his lusterless eyes, unfathomably sad, beamed in a sort of rapture and his withered hands made abortive, convulsive movements; suddenly he slumped down in a fit, and the warder put him back to bed.

That evening a young lady doctor came round the ward; her glasses glittered in a friendly manner. When she came to me I asked her in a low voice for a sleeping draught; I did not know, I said, whether my nerves would stand another sleepless night. Her glasses flashed angrily:

"So that's your game! First betray your country and then whimper for sleeping draughts!"

She bent over the bed of a complete idiot:

"But you were at the front, weren't you, Herr Schmidt? You wouldn't sell yourself to the enemy?"

Herr Schmidt answered with a vacant stare.

One should not ask too much of doctors. If they are clever they soon pick up the traditional old wives' cures and serve them up with very much the same effect that charms and amulets and magic incantations produced in earlier days. They know nothing of your real sufferings, and even if they do know they don't understand.

The head of the Munich clinic was the celebrated Professor Krapelin who founded (in a Munich *bierkeller*) a society to encompass the downfall of England.

He held forth at length to me. "How can you dare deny Germany's just claims to power?" he said. "We shall win this war. Germany needs room for expansion—she needs Belgium and the Baltic Provinces. Paris would have been in our hands long ago but for you and your like. It is you who are delaying our victory."

He went red in the face in his efforts to convince me of the necessity of the pan-German outlook. I realized that there were two kinds of sick men: the harmless ones lay in barred and bolted rooms and were called lunatics; the dangerous ones proved that hunger was good for a nation and founded societies

135

to encompass the downfall of England—these were allowed to lock up those other poor harmless ones.

"We speak different languages, sir," I said at last. "Possibly I understand your language, but mine is certainly Greek to you."

"We shall not detain you longer than necessary," he snapped.

They let me out after four days, and I thanked my lucky stars. Some weeks later, in the summer of 1918, I was discharged from the barracks and left for Berlin.

10. Revolution

Germany's needs became ever more bitter. The bread grew still worse, the milk still thinner; the farmers would have nothing to do with the towns and would-be hoarders came back empty-handed; the men at the front were incensed at the debauchery and gormandizing at the Base and at the misery at home. They had had enough. "Equal food and equal pay, and the Frenchies would soon be chased away," they sang.

For four years they had fought, on the eastern front, on the western front, in Asia, in Africa; for four years they had stood their ground in the rain and mud of Flanders, in the poisonous mists of the Wollonian swamps, in the scorching blaze of Mesopotamia.

During the night of October 3rd the Peace Note was despatched to President Wilson.

This unexpected bid for peace opened the eyes of the German people at last; they had had no idea of the impending catastrophe. So it was all for nothing— the millions of dead, the millions of wounded, the starvation at home. All for nothing.

The triumph of the bourgeois democracy which accompanied the move for Peace aroused no interest, neither the Reichstag nor the people opposed it. It came into being like ration cards, like turnip jam. And anyway, what obvious changes did it make? The old, privileged electorate was abolished. Liebknecht and the other political prisoners were amnestied. But the press was still censored; the right to hold meetings was still denied; the Generals had still the ruling voice in everything; the Ministers came from the old ruling caste. Scheidemann and Bauer, the Social Democrats, were Secretaries of State. Excellencies. Good God!

The people thought only of peace. They had been thinking of war too long, believing in victory too long. Why hadn't they been told the truth? Why hadn't they been told when even the war-lords desponded? How could the people help despairing?

The men who ruled them, the men who had driven them for years on end with blind authority and had completely lost touch with them, had, indeed, noticed this anxiety, this tiredness, this despair; but they had no thought for anything but the Monarchy and the danger to the Monarch. We can still save the Monarchy, they thought, if the Kaiser abdicates. The people consigned the Monarchy to hell; they had been lost to Wilhelm for a long, long time. The question was no longer Wilhelm or another Kaiser, but war or peace.

The sailors of the Fleet, the Kaiser's own men,

were the first to revolt. The High Seas Fleet was to have put to sea. The officers preferred "death with honor to peace with ignominy." But the men, who had already begun to revolt in 1917, refused to put to sea. They drew the furnaces. Six hundred were arrested; the others abandoned their ships, stormed the prisons, and took possession of Kiel. The dockers joined them. The German Revolution had begun.

First Kiel, then Munich, then Hanover, Hamburg, the Rhineland, Berlin. On November 9th, 1918, the Berlin workers left the factories and marched in thousands from north, south and east to the center of the city—old gray men and women who had stood for years at the munition benches, men invalided out of the army, boys who had taken over their fathers' work. The processions were joined by men on leave, war-widows, wounded soldiers, students and solid citizens. No leader had arranged this uprising. The Revolutionary leaders at the factories had reckoned on a later day. The Social Democratic Deputies were surprised and dismayed. They were even then discussing ways and means of saving the Monarchy with the Chancellor, Prince Max of Baden.

The procession marched on in silence; there was no singing, no rejoicing. It came to a standstill before the gates of the Maikäfer Barracks. The gates were barred; rifles and machine guns threatened from every window and loophole. Would the soldiers shoot?

But the men in field gray were the brothers of these ragged, starving crowds. They flung down their weapons, the gates were opened and the people streamed into the barracks and joined forces with the Kaiser's army.

The Imperial standard was hauled down and the Red flag fluttered in its place. From the balcony of the Imperial Palace Liebknecht proclaimed the German Socialist Republic.

The ruling powers gave in without a struggle, the officers surrendered. Only one officer in the whole of Germany, the captain of the *König*, remained loyal to his Kaiser and died for him. And the aristocracy? Prince Heinrich, the Kaiser's brother, sewed a red band on his sleeve and fled. The Bavarian Crown Prince, Rupprecht, abandoned his troops in the red-flagged car of the Brussels Soldiers' Council. Wilhelm II fled to Holland. A pitiful debacle, but dangerous for the people. They wanted peace, and what they got was power, which fell into their hands without a struggle. Would they learn to keep their power?

The Crown Princess was waiting in the Palace at Potsdam. She had gathered her children round her and thought of the fate of Marie Antoinette, of the fate of the Tsaritza. Soon the Revolutionaries would storm the Palace and make away with her and her children. An old servant came to her and in a quavering voice announced that the Revolutionary Soldiers'

Council of Potsdam wished to speak to her Imperial Highness. The Soldiers' Councilor entered the room and clicked his heels. He had not come to make an arrest. He spoke deferentially: In the name of the Potsdam Soldiers' Council he was to ask her Imperial Highness whether her Imperial Highness felt safe enough, and to report that in any case the Potsdam Council had detailed ten Revolutionary soldiers for the protection of her Imperial Highness. He clicked his heels once more and departed.

No fairy-tale. The second son of the Crown Princess told it to me himself. "It was typical of your whole Revolution," he said.

In Hamburg the Independents took possession of the building of the Social Democratic newspaper. The Democrats ran for help to an old Imperial judge, who exercised the authority he no longer possessed. They rushed back to the building with the signed paper, and when the Independent Revolutionaries read it, and saw the seal of authority, furious but alarmed they withdrew.

The German Revolution found an ignorant people and an Official class of bureaucratic Philistines. The people shouted for Socialism, yet they had no clear conception of what Socialism should be. They recognized their oppressors; they knew well enough what they did not want; but they had little idea of what they did want. The Social Democrats and the Trades Union leaders were linked by blood and friendship with the representatives of the Monarchy and of capitalism, whose sins were their sins. They were satisfied with the *juste milieu* of the bourgeois; their ideal was the overthrow of the proletariat by the strengthening of the petty bourgeoisie. They had no faith in the doctrines which they had proclaimed, no faith in the people who trusted them.

Immediately after the Revolution they opened fire —not on the enemies of the Revolution; no. On their own most ardent pioneers. They harassed and persecuted them until they had them down and then basked in the applause of fashionable drawing rooms. They hated the Revolution. Ebert had the courage to say so outright.

The people, to whom the Monarchy had forbidden any control of their own destiny, now renounced it of their own accord. Instead of destroying the old reactionary bureaucracy they pampered it and tended it, and were snapped at for their pains.

In the first few days the army officers had their tabs torn from their shoulders; the people did not want to hurt them, they merely wanted to destroy the symbols of authority, recognizing with a sure instinct that the strength of the ruling classes lay in symbols, traditions, inbred feelings. It was not long before the officers bobbed up again.

I arrived in Berlin at the end of October, and spoke at meetings for a mass uprising in opposition to Walter Rathenau's call for national resistance. Even if an individual may claim the right to suicide it is fantastic nonsense that a whole people should rush to death in emulation of their leader. Implicit in Rathenau's appeal was the wholesale self-destruction of Germany. We who had been Heidelberg students, older and wiser now, found our feet once more and united to combat this delirium. We saw the Revolution coming, and prepared ourselves.

On November 9th I was in bed with a bad attack of influenza at my mother's house at Landsberg. While the doctor was observing my growing fever with a thoughtful expression my sister came in with the news of the Revolution. Next day I was on the way to Berlin.

Hugo Haase, the People's Commissioner, had suggested that I should go to Munich as secretary to Georg von Arco, the representative of the new Republic there. But before that came about Eisner himself adopted me.

The Bavarians also were tired of war, and to their weariness was added the fear that the Italian troops might march on Bavaria after the collapse of Austria. The Bavarians had seen war in France and Russia; they remembered shell-churned trenches, devastated villages, a land laid waste. The old traditional hatred of the Prussians, the Hohenzollerns, reawoke. The Prussians could get on with the war as best they could by themselves. As for the Royal House of Wittelsbach, there was nothing more to be expected. The King, said the peasants, had got himself thor-

143

oughly tied up with Berlin; otherwise he would have insisted on the farmers' rights before now; instead of which they weren't allowed to grind their own corn, and, just because the Prussian swine didn't mind bad beer, the Bavarians also had to swallow dish-water.

Eisner, with uncanny acuteness, divined the mood of the country, and won over peasants and workers to his side to overthrow the Monarchy and resist the Social Democrats who were then drawing up a new constitution.

Kiel was the beacon. On November 7th two hundred thousand people, led by Eisner and the blind farmer Gandorfer, assembled in the Theresienwiese and marched on the city. The King fled and Bavaria was in the hands of the Revolutionaries. That night the Workers' and Soldiers' Councils elected Eisner President of the Bavarian Free State.

I myself was elected deputy President by the Central Committee of the Workmen's, Peasants' and Soldiers' Councils, among whom I found many friends of the January strike. In the routine work of the days that followed I came to understand the thousand and one practical needs of peasants and workers.

In mid-December I went to Berlin for the Congress of all Councils. Here at last, I thought, the political will of the German Revolution will make itself known. But what instability, what ignorance, what an utter lack of any will to power that Congress showed!

The German Congress of Councils voluntarily renounced all the power that the Revolution had thrust so unexpectedly into their hands. They threw it overboard and left the fate of the Republic to the chance results of a questionable election and an ignorant people. In every parliamentary Republic, the Congress decided, the Ministers are responsible to the parliament; the People's Commissioners,· therefore, must rule independently of the control and will of the Central Council. The Republic had passed its own death-sentence.

When Karl Liebknecht and Rosa Luxemburg, the pioneers of the Revolution, tried to address the Congress, they were refused a hearing.

A month later the Spartacus rebellion broke out, against the will of Liebknecht and Rosa Luxemburg; and both were killed. "Shot while attempting to escape" ran the official report. The news reached me in Munich and I forced my way into a mass meeting of the Social Democrats. "Liebknecht and Luxemburg have been murdered!" I shouted. The crowd, the deluded crowd, shouted back: "Serve them right! Why couldn't they leave well enough alone?"

In Bavaria the forces of reaction hindered the activity of the various Councils. They found allies among the Social Democratic ministers, and an armed Defense Corps was formed with the help of Auer. This Defense Corps was the first fruit of the counter-revolutionaries, forerunner of the *Orgesch*, of the

Stahlhelm, of the *Einwohnerwehr,* of the National Socialist Storm Troops. The day was to come when they would turn on those who brought them into being. Side by side with the official Corps other un-official corps grew up. A group of manufacturers financed a band of mercenaries; the officers of the old régime were in their element again, hatching plots to seize the Government buildings; organizing spy agencies and *Sprengkommandos* and elaborate systems of defensive alarm. When they struck they would proclaim that they were saving the National Assem-bly from the Bolsheviks; actually their *Putsch* would mean the overthrow of the Republic. Their plans were betrayed to us, and the Workers' Council ordered me to disclose them to the Provisional Na-tional Council. The Defense Corps went on with its secret work, the results of which were soon to appear.

At the beginning of February I accompanied Eisner to the Congress of the Second International at Berne. What fervent hopes were placed on this International by the proletariat of every land!

Never again would it be possible for the lords of capitalism to stir up war and delude the peoples; never again would the people believe in fairy-tales of "attacking" and "attacked" countries! The peoples of the world were no longer credulous enough to follow their rulers like sheep; their eyes had been opened.

146

The original Second International had broken up on August 4th, 1914, the first day of the war; neither the leaders nor the people themselves stood by it; only a little group remained faithful to their ideals. In face of the feverish spread of wartime nationalism nobody remembered to think internationally; chauvinism triumphed; the proletariat of every land forgot their oaths of brotherhood and shot each other down. They rushed to the defense not of humanity but of the capitalistic states; their enemies were no longer the bourgeois but their friends on the wrong side of the border; the ideals of the past were stronger than those of the future; the instincts so long instilled by the ruling classes proved stronger than their transient reasoned ideas.

The survivors of the wreck of the old Second International met again in Berne; but they lacked the courage to acknowledge their bankruptcy, or to inquire into the political, moral, and psychological causes of this bankruptcy. They wrangled day after day over the question of war-guilt; ministers of munitions, royal Socialists, militaristic Social Democrats, piled reproaches on one another's heads; each concentrated on the sins of the others and forgot his own. Friedrich Adler and a few others who had avowed their Socialism throughout the war did their best to save this new Second International. But the Manifesto of Unity could not conceal the hopeless underlying division. Parties who could literally have conquered the world voluntarily sounded their own death-knell. It

147

was the shattering of a tremendous faith, a tremendous hope for humanity. It left a need for a new foundation, for new forms, new ways.

In his speech at Berne against imperialism and the criminals who had brought war upon us, Eisner had aroused the bitter hatred of the German reactionaries. On his way to the opening of the Bavarian Diet he was shot down by the twenty-one-year-old Graf Arco-Valley.

The Landtag was opened. Suddenly a worker, Alois Lindner, rushed into the hall, cried that Auer was behind Eisner's murder, and fired. Auer dropped, severely wounded, to the floor. The Deputies scattered panic-stricken, leaving behind them their Parliament, their people, their mandate, and their hats. Bavaria had no Government.

I had gone on from the Conference of Berne to spend a few days with friends in the Engadine, and there, at St. Moritz, I watched the *jeunesse dorée* of every land, fashionable, bejeweled, playing at happiness like the ghosts and lemures of a forgotten world.

On February 21st, 1919, I returned to Bavaria. At one of the stations I heard a Swiss porter outside shouting excitedly, and in the carriage a German commercial traveler started cheering. I could not take in the words that were beating into my head; but at last I forced myself to realize—Kurt Eisner had been murdered.

Eisner was a man of an entirely different mold from the Eberts, the Scheidemanns, the Noskes and

148

Auers. In him was embodied all that is finest in Nordic austerity and Latin rationalism. His political idea was the complete democracy. He had no use for the parliamentary democracy which once in a while summons the people to the ballot box and then loses all touch with them for years on end. The spirit of life and of truth, he urged, should permeate the whole social structure as a critical, invigorating, and fiery spirit to influence the communal daily life. Believing this, Eisner put his faith in a Soviet Republic. But even he did not perceive the necessity for the rapid erection of a new social structure. At the head of the Commission of Socialization which the Congress of Councils had asked for, he placed Professor Brentano, the well-known exponent of free-trade. In the first session Brentano made a pronouncement which caused the industrial magnates to sit up; industry can only be socialized, he said, when it is already in existence, and in Germany today it is non-existent.

Eisner loathed the Press as a deluder of the people, although when some Revolutionaries seized the editorship of one of the worst papers he personally went to the newspaper office and forced the invaders to retreat—so great was his contempt for journalism, so great his respect for the formal freedom of the Press. "Truth," he wrote during the war in a memoradum to the Munich General Command, "is the greatest of all national possessions. A state, a people, a system, which suppresses the truth or fears to publish it, deserves to collapse as rapidly and completely as possible."

Eisner, the moralist, fought against developments in Berlin. He believed that the responsible officials of the superseded system, who were still working in the Foreign Office and conducting negotiations with the Entente, were putting obstacles in the way of peace; that new men, upright Republicans who had had no share in the guilt of the Monarchy, ought to be installed in their place and would be able to obtain better terms for Germany. He cherished the illusion that Clemenceau was a pioneer of European democracy, and greatly wished to speak with him personally, to convince him that the German people had achieved freedom and responsibility with their Revolution, and that it would be a crime against Europe to abase the German people with a cruel peace. Clemenceau, however, rebuffed the go-between and actually threatened to arrest him for "conspiring with the enemy." The French politicians and militarists would have nothing to do with the German Revolution: some regarded it as a subterfuge on the part of the fallen Monarchy, others regarded it as a triumph of Bolshevism, and feared the infection of France herself.

All his life Eisner had been poor, self-sufficient, and detached. He was small and slight; gray hair that had once been fair fell in a confused tangle to his coat-collar, and an untidy beard straggled over his chest; short-sighted eyes looked out calmly from the deeply lined face. His small, feminine, well-kept hands responded to the grip neither of friends nor of enemies, a characteristic which indicated his shyness of all human relationship.

The thing which differentiated him from all the other Republican ministers was his will to action; his unflinching courage. He knew that a nation, like a human being, matures only in daily work; that it cannot develop if a wall is raised between life and action. And he did not fear death. The people felt this, and believed in him because of it. Talents are given to many, but the masses will follow only those whom they know have overcome the fear of death.

11. The Bavarian Soviet Republic

The shot fired by Arco shook the whole Republic, and the people clamored for revenge for Eisner's death. The Central Committee of the Workmen's, Peasants' and Soldiers' Councils took over the government, proclaimed a general strike and a state of siege throughout Bavaria. It convened the Congress of the Councils; and the working classes, disappointed by the inactivity of the Republic, demanded that their politicians should embrace the Revolution once and for all, crying that what had succeeded in Russia would also succeed in Bavaria, and that parliamentary government was a wash-out: the idea of a Soviet Republic had swept the masses.

Up to now the Communist Party had been practically impotent, with little or no influence; but now their slogans became popular. The Communist Central Office in Berlin sent Leviné to Munich. Leviné had already fought as a student in the Russian Revolution of 1905; had been arrested, imprisoned in the Schlüsselburg, and banished to a lead mine in Siberia, whence he had escaped to Europe via Asia, to study economics in Germany. In 1918 he joined the Spartacists. This haggard figure, with his arched, fleshy nose jutting out from the sunken cheeks, was nothing of a demagogue; every time he spoke he had to fight for attention, to compel it with infrequent gesture and incisive argument. In a few weeks he had reorganized the party and settled its political attitude.

At that time I was due to take part in a conference of the Independent Socialists in Berlin. Delayed by work at the Central Council, I had missed my train; so I decided to go by air the next morning.

My pilot was an army pilot, decorated with the Iron Cross First-Class and bar. When we set off the blue sky had a southern intensity. I sat behind the pilot in a tiny cramped seat; a square hole in the floor through which they dropped bombs in wartime served now as a window through which I could watch the receding earth. It was my first flight. The black forests, green fields, brown hills and deep valleys were neat, flat, colored squares, like children's colored bricks. On every side towered great mountains of cloud. The earth was soon veiled by a soft white layer of mist; and I was seized by a horrible impulse to fling myself through it, to feel myself falling.

The clouds vanished, the sun was at the zenith; I looked at my watch and saw that we had been flying for some hours and were already due at Leipzig, where the pilot was to take in more fuel.

153

I handed him a little note: "When do we get to Leipzig?"

He shrugged his shoulders. He had lost his way.

Suddenly the engine gave out and we began to glide down; then, before I could strap myself in, we had got into a spin and nose-dived into a field. I was sent flying, caught my head on the edge of the fuselage and lost consciousness. When I came to, some peasants had come up, and we found we had landed not in Leipzig but in Vilshofen in Lower Bavaria.

The peasants helped us, and we found that the aeroplane was not badly damaged.

"Can we go on to Berlin?" I asked the pilot.

"No."

"What are we to do, then?"

"I can get back to Munich all right, but I won't be responsible for you."

"I'll come with you on my own responsibility."

We arrived at Munich that evening without further mishap, and the next morning, very early, I set out with another pilot in another aeroplane. The sky was overcast, with frequent drenching showers. Hour after hour we flew on without a sight of Leipzig. I remembered yesterday's crash and buckled myself firmly to my seat. A few minutes later we lost height and landed in a sodden, muddy field, bumped along for a few yards and then capsized in a hollow. I hung upside down in my straps while the pilot climbed out with blood streaming from mouth and nose.

"Nothing to worry about," he called, and pulled me out from under the aeroplane.

Not far off we saw a village, and peasants came rushing up. They weren't at all concerned about us, but carried bottles, saucepans, pails, every conceivable sort of receptacle large or small, to catch the petrol which poured out of the tank; for in those days petrol was dearer than gold, dearer than life.

The pilot and I stumbled along to the village in our heavy flying suits and found an inn, where we lay down on benches and, exhausted by the shock, fell asleep at once. I must have slept for hours, for when I awoke it was dusk. Hazily I was aware of peasants sitting round the bare tables. I got up, and saw a policeman standing at the door.

"Nothing doing, froggy!" he called out, and signaled that he wouldn't let me outside.

"But I'm a German!" And I pulled my papers out of my pocket and handed them over. He opened his eyes when he saw them, and beckoned me to follow him outside.

"So you're Herr Toller, are you! You take my tip and don't let on as to who you are. These fellows here think you're a froggy. Let 'em think it. If they knew you was a Red they'd knobble you on the spot. We don't encourage Reds here in Wertheim."

I took the narrow-gauge railway to Ingolstadt.

"Is there another train today to Munich?" I asked the station master.

"Aye."

"I must take it then."

"Not that, you won't."

"Why not?"

"It's a special, and it won't stop here."

"What special?"

"Taking the Diet to Munich."

"We'll have to stop it, then."

"That train wouldn't stop here if you was King of Bavaria."

"I'm not the King of Bavaria." And I showed him my papers.

"Well, it's no concern of mine."

"I see," I said, and putting my hand in my pocket I clenched it round my handkerchief as though it were a revolver and repeated fiercely:

"You will stop that train!"

He shrank visibly under my gaze, squirming; then drew himself up, stuck out his chest, touched his cap, and murmured:

"Yes, sir."

Ten minutes later I boarded the Munich train; it was too late to go to the Berlin conference now. If I had got there, there I should have had to stay; for two days later war broke out between Berlin and Munich.

Before the Bavarian Diet could start work the Augsburg workers, weary of Revolutionary resolutions and proposals, sent a delegation to Munich to demand the proclamation of a Soviet Republic. The Government did not arrest these men for High Treason; instead it listened to them peaceably. The Social Democratic ministers lost their heads; in a frantic effort to retain office they were prepared to yield to all demands. One of them, President Hoffmann, was unavoidably absent; he wrote an anxious postcard to the chairman of the Central Committee asking whether the Soviet Republic would pension former ministers.

The Communists remained aloof; they distrusted the Social Democrats who, as so often before in this Revolution, were pursuing a shady game of their own, a dangerous game for the workers. Besides, they said, the workers were not yet ready, and without the support of North Germany a Soviet Republic could not hope to last. But they should have said that earlier, in the days when they were frantically demanding a Soviet Republic and stigmatizing as counter-revolutionary anybody who doubted its possibility. It is no good making pronouncements in which one does not believe, for dislike of the truth often leads to self-betrayal. And it is no good shrinking from reality when it happens to turn out a little different from what one had hoped.

The Independent Socialists hesitated. Had a revolutionary party the right to leave the people in the lurch? Revolutionary leaders should not blindly follow the whims of the masses; they should guard against making mistakes. But was this merely a whim?

Wasn't it already a *fait accompli*, only the results of which we could influence? The party leaders advise, but it is the people who act. At that moment the Soviet Republic was already proclaimed in Würzburg, Augsburg, Fürth, Aschaffenburg, Lindau and Hof. Long before this we should have enlightened the people as to the true balance of power in Germany; we had only ourselves to blame if they did not fully understand how things stood.

On the night of April 17th, 1919, the Central Committee delegates from the various Socialist parties, from the Trades Unions and the Farmers' Union, assembled in the Wittelsbach Palace. The great rooms where once maids-in-waiting and powdered lackeys had fawned attendance on their royal masters now rang with the heavy tread of workmen, farmers and soldiers. Red Guards, couriers, and typists leaned out from the silk-curtained windows of the ex-Queen's bedroom.

The People's Commissaries were elected, and even here the ignorance, aimlessness, and general vagueness of the German Revolution were manifest. Men with diametrically opposed views on finance and economics were appointed to responsible positions, men whom nobody could expect to work together. Three men were put up to me for People's Commissaries, and one after another I had to turn them down. Dr. Lipp, a man of completely unknown qualifications, was proposed as chief People's Commissary for For-

158

eign Affairs. His face was all beard; his suit all frock-coat; these two requisites seemed to be the sum total of his accomplishments. A workman whom I asked about Dr. Lipp said that he was a personal friend of the Pope's. Other men were entrusted with office who could hardly have boasted acquaintanceship with a parish priest.

As I left the Wittelsbach Palace the new day was dawning. The Revolution was an established fact. But—was it? This Soviet Republic was a foolhardy *coup de main* on the part of the bewildered workers, an attempt to salvage the lost German Revolution. What would it achieve? How would it end?

Outside the little hotel where I was living one of our Section leaders was waiting.

"At last we have got the power into our hands," he said.

"You think we have?" I answered. He started at that, stared at me thoughtfully, and I left him abruptly.

The first day of the Soviet Republic: a general holiday. Workers, self-conscious in their best clothes, crowded the fashionable streets, talking of last night's happenings. Heavy lorries crowded with soldiers patrolled the city, and the Red Flag streamed over the Wittelsbach Palace.

Work began in earnest. Edicts were issued, proclaiming the socialization of the Press, the arming of workmen and the institution of a Red Army, the

159

State control of houses to alleviate the housing shortage, and the State regulation of food supplies.

The Munich garrison despatched representatives to the Central Committee, to declare their loyalty to the Republic. The men of the First Life Guards renamed their barracks after Karl Liebknecht. Even the old Imperial lawyers and judges were unwilling to retire, and decided to stand by the Soviet, quite prepared to prosecute the enemies of the Revolution in the new Revolutionary Courts. All the church bells were set ringing for the Republic.

Only the Communists still opposed the Soviet. They summoned the workers to demonstrations and sent speakers to the barracks to prove that this Republic was not worthy of a soldier's defense.

Meanwhile President Hoffmann and the other Ministers who had fled from Munich pulled themselves together; the Government formed by the Diet removed to Bamberg and called on Epp's army in Ohrdruf to protect them. They arrested supporters of the Soviet Republic and ruled all Northern Bavaria.

In Munich the President of the Central Committee retired, and I was appointed his successor.

All day long people crowded the anteroom waiting their turn to see me. Each one of them believed that the Soviet Republic had been expressly created to satisfy his own private desires. A woman wanted to get married at once; up to now there had been difficulties, for she lacked the necessary papers, but obviously the Soviet Republic had been instituted for the sole purpose of salvaging her personal happiness. A man wanted me to force his landlord to remit his rent. A group of supporters of the Revolution came to demand the arrest of their own particular enemies.

Unappreciated cranks submitted their programs for the betterment of humanity, believing that at last their much-scorned ideas would have a chance to turn earth into Paradise. They all had their own infallible and omnipotent cures; and, granted their premises, their logic was unimpeachable. Some believed that the root of all evil was cooked food, others the gold standard, others unhygienic underwear, or machinery, or the lack of a compulsory universal language, or multiple stores, or birth control. They reminded me of the Swabian shoemaker who wrote a voluminous pamphlet to prove that man owed his moral sickness to the fact that he satisfied his elementary needs in closed rooms and with the aid of artificial paper; whereas if he spent these daily moments out in the woods and availed himself of the natural moss all spiritual poisons would also evaporate into the surrounding air, and he would be at the same time bodily and spiritually purified, returning to his work with a strengthened social conscience and a diminished egoism; true love of humanity would be awakened and the Kingdom of God on Earth would be at hand.

The Commissary for Foreign Affairs, Dr. Lipp, was already exercising his prerogatives. He broadcasted

161

despatches right and left; apparently he really did know the Pope, for he telegraphed to the Nuncio:

"I shall make it my Holy Duty to guarantee the safety of your Reverence and of the whole of your entourage in Munich. Rest assured of my devotion."

Our control officials in the telegraph office shook their heads over his despatches, which became ever more high-flown. One day they brought me a telegram addressed to the Pope and asked me if the Central Committee had sanctioned its despatch. I read:

"Proletariat of Upper Bavaria happily united. Socialists plus Independents plus Communists firmly as one, together with Farmers' Union. Liberal bourgeoisie completely disarmed as Prussian agents. Cowardly Hoffmann, who took away the key of my W.C. in his flight, now established at Bamberg. Prussian politicians, aided by Hoffmann, attempting to cut us off from the North, Berlin, Leipzig, Nürnberg, also from Frankfurt and the Essen coal-mines; also stigmatizing us to the Entente as bloodhounds and looters. In that I see the bloody hand of Gustav Noske. Receiving coal and food in tremendous quantities from Switzerland and Italy. We want peace forever. Immanuel Kant, *Vom Ewigen Frieden*, 1795, theses 2-5. Prussia only wants the Armistice to prepare for her revenge."

Without a doubt Lipp had gone off his head. We decided to send him immediately to a sanatorium, and to avoid a public sensation, to ask him to resign voluntarily.

162

In the Ministry for the Exterior the typists' rooms were all blooming with red carnations; Dr. Lipp had brought them in that morning and then gone out again, nobody knew where. Doubtless he was sending off further despatches. At last we managed to run him to earth; he came to my room in the Palace utterly ignorant of what was in store for him.

"Have you seen the King's bathroom?" he asked. "I tell you it's a scandal. I found a little boat there and the lackeys told me that instead of governing King Ludwig used to sit in a hot bath for hours on end playing with his little boat."

I knew all about the ex-King's bathroom; but at the moment I had more serious things to talk about.

"Are you responsible for this telegram?" I asked.

Lipp carefully read the telegram through and announced that he had written it with his own hand.

"You will have to resign. We have already drawn up the text of your explanation; and perhaps you would be so good as to put your signature to it."

Lipp rose from his chair, settled the lapels of his frock-coat, took out a comb and with studied gestures rearranged his Henri Quatre beard; then, replacing the comb, he took up the pen, and, leaning for a moment on the writing table, murmured sadly:

"Even this will I do for the Republic."

Then he signed the document and departed.

That same afternoon he was back at the office, giving flowers to the typists and despatching more telegrams. He was kindly but firmly taken away.

On April 9th one of our Section leaders burst into my room.

"The Communists have elected their own Revolutionary Foremen in the factories and called them to a meeting in the *Mattäserkeller*. We are to be chucked out tonight."

I shook my head incredulously. Had not the Communists themselves opposed the creation of the Soviet Republic, prophesying, and rightly too, that if it collapsed the consequences to the workers would be disastrous? What could have decided them to make a bid for power now? The position was just the same as it had been a few days back, if anything still more precarious. It was simply that the Communist Party did not like being a minority party in any government; although they were not the workers' leaders, they demanded a front place in the Government, from which they could dictate their wishes.

Leviné was speaking when I arrived at the *Mattäserkeller*. The Soviet Republic was only a pseudo Soviet, he declared. The Government was not fit to govern and must be overthrown to make room for a new Central Council.

The meeting was absolutely with Leviné.

I tried in vain to catch the chairman's eye, so at last I appealed to the people, and they demanded that I should be given a chance to speak. The Central Council which they were going to overthrow had been elected by the Congress of Workmen's, Peasants' and Soldiers' Councils, supported by the Farmers' Union.

"If you have revised your political opinion," I cried, "and really believe now that the present confusion is due solely to the incompetence of the Government, then it is up to you to coöperate in saving the Revolution. If you overthrow us and set up a new government without the support of the peasants, where will you be? How will you feed the city?"

"We'll do what they do in Russia," answered Leviné. "We'll carry class warfare into the villages. We'll send punitive expeditions to force the peasants to deliver grain and milk."

"Those expeditions never met with the least success in Russia," I said, "and in Bavaria they would be a complete fiasco. In Bavaria you can't base your plans on the poverty of the peasants; even the Lower Bavarian landowners are no Russian Moujiks. The Bavarian peasant is utterly different from the Russian peasant. He is armed, and he would put up a strong fight. Do you want to go to war about every gallon of milk?"

The meeting was with me now.

Then another Communist got up, and the meeting was with *him*. The secretary of the Communist Party was to go to the Palace and kindly explain to the Government that it had fallen.

The meeting elected a new Government, none of the members of which, apart from the Communist leaders, I had ever heard of. Some of them were

165

nominated because they were Social Democrats: so that what had been a crime with us—cöoperation with the Social Democrats—was now hailed as a great virtue! Whether these men were competent or incompetent, and whether they had any influence in their party, did not seem to matter at all.

The meeting then passed a manifesto calling out the workmen of Munich in a general strike and demanding the disarming of the various Munich armies and of the police.

The new Government went home. I remained; I was under arrest.

Couriers came and went, committees were organized, proclamations were drawn up and sealed—with considerable foresight they had brought with them the seal of the new Council.

The tables were still crowded, sleepy waiters served beer and sausages; the noise of conversation gradually died down, gestures flagged, the stale air was thick with smoke.

At two in the morning there was a sudden hubbub outside, the doors burst open, and a body of soldiers of the Republican *Schutztruppe* rushed into the hall with rifles and revolvers. The commander forced a way for himself through the crowd, making straight for me. I flinched back. He shouted at me:

"We've come to take you away!"

The crowd did not know whether the raid was on their account or mine until the commander turned and covering them with his revolver yelled:

166

"Hands up! Clear out! Anyone here after this drum ceases will be shot!"

The drum was already rolling out, the crowd was surrounded by armed soldiers, and hundreds of rifle barrels gleamed threateningly. Some of the workers dashed for the windows and jumped out; but most of them stayed where they were.

"Shoot if you've got the guts to!"

I caught the commander's arm:

"Have you gone out of your senses? Cancel that order at once! Tell them you don't mean it!"

"No."

"Then I'll have to."

Trembling with rage the man leveled his revolver at me; but I had already shouted:

"It's all right. Nobody's going to shoot!"

Then the soldiers withdrew, taking me with them to the City Commandant.

"The troops know that the Communists intend to disarm them," the Commandant said. "All the barracks have been notified and strengthened; if the workers try to storm the barracks they'll get a warm welcome. There'll be bloodshed in Munich today."

When I left the Commandant it was six in the morning and I saw the first trams: evidently the drivers had not responded to the call to strike.

I went to Krupp's and another big steel works and spoke to mass meetings of the men, and persuaded them not to join in the march on the barracks. The other factories also decided not to follow the Communists.

The new Government dispersed. A few hours later not a soul remembered that it had ever existed; not even the Communist Party.

While the Revolutionaries were bickering amongst themselves in Munich their opponents in the North were uniting. Schneppenhorst, who only a week before had pledged his life in defense of the Soviet Republic, was forming an army to overthrow us. The internal strife in Munich had to be ended at once. The Central Council exhorted the Communists once again, pointing out that their coöperation was necessary to save the Revolution—regardless of party conflicts. The Communists sent delegates to the Council, but they came too late.

The Soviet Republic was doomed. The inadequacy of its leaders, the opposition of the Communists, the secession of the Social Democrats, the disorganization of the administration, the increasing food-shortage, the confusion among the armed forces —all these circumstances hastened collapse and gave power to the rapidly growing counter-revolutionary movement.

In my political inexperience I dared not reveal the true position in all its harshness to the workers.

But the politician's worst crime is silence. He must speak the truth, however unpalatable; the truth alone can spur on strength and will and reason.

168

This Soviet Republic was a failure, and the only thing to do with failures is to acknowledge them freely and discard them. Already the Soldiers' Councils were negotiating with the Social Democrats of their own accord. We had no time to lose: counter-revolutionary activity was striking at us from our midst.

On Saturday April 12th the telephone rang.

"Is this Toller?" asked a voice.

"Yes, who's this?"

"That's neither here nor there. I'm telephoning to warn you that they're preparing a *Putsch* against the Soviet."

That was all. I tried to ask more, but he had replaced the receiver. Our position was too precarious as it was for me to ignore this 'phone call. I gave the alarm to the night-shifts in the great factories.

Acting on a vague premonition I did not go home that night, but slept at a friend's flat.

I awoke next morning to hear him telephoning. He nodded to me as he repeated the message he had just received.

"*Putsch* against the Soviet succeeding . . . Hoffmann's troops occupying the station . . . all the members of the Central Council arrested . . . Mühsam, Hagemeister . . . Wadler . . . Only Toller and Leviné not yet rounded up, but we're already hot on their trail."

My friend hung up the receiver, and simultaneously the doorbell rang.

My friend started and looked at me enquiringly.

"They've run me to earth," I thought, and wondered what on earth to do.

"It's too late to get away," he said.

The bell rang again.

"There is a sort of cupboard behind the bookcase. Help me move it so that you can hide."

I squeezed into the hole and my friend pushed back the bookcase.

After a time he came to let me out.

"You're in luck's way!" he said. "It's a young subaltern; but he is just back from the East and says he's fed up with the Monarchy and now the Kaiser's run away he won't have anything to do with it. And anyway he wasn't looking for Socialists but for a woman, and he regards all politicians, Right or Left, with equal loathing. I managed to get some news out of him."

In the first place Hoffmann had won over the Republican *Schutztruppe* with the help of the Munich Social Democrats and a promise of 300 marks to every man. In the second place the station and Government buildings were in the hands of his army which was master of the whole city. The Soviet had gone down ingloriously.

Although the workers had proved too weak to build up a lasting government they were not going to hand over the city to the Whites without any resistance. They gathered in the Theresienwiese, joined forces with the Revolutionary troops, and the fight began.

The street outside the house was being patrolled by men from Hoffmann's army. I asked the subaltern to lend me his uniform.

"With pleasure," he said. "You can have the whole outfit complete with orders and ribbons. On one condition. When you get back into power again you must give me an aeroplane so that I can fly to the North Pole and marry an Eskimo girl and forget the whole bloody lot of you."

"It's a long way to go," I said.

"It's well worth it," he answered. "These European women are all a lot of frustrated soldiers. I want to marry a woman, not a spiritual sergeant-major."

I rigged myself up in his uniform and went out into the street.

The White soldiers I met saluted me.

A workman, shouldering a rifle, ran into me.

"Where's the fighting, comrade?" I said.

He stopped short, stared at me and my lieutenant's uniform and pulled a face: "Holy Moses!"

I repeated my question.

He raised his rifle, aimed, dropped it again.

"Get on with you!" he said.

I had forgotten all about my uniform. I remembered and made myself scarce.

Meanwhile the Revolutionaries had won back the station, and the Whites had retreated in the trains which had been kept under steam.

The only place still held by the Whites was the high-school in the Luitpoldstrasse. My worker friends and I rushed the place and the soldiers surrendered.

While I was away fighting, the Factory Councils had assembled, and, believing that the whole of the old Central Council had been arrested, elected a new one, predominantly Communist. I went to the Town Commandant's office where the new Council was sitting, but before I could open my mouth I was arrested. "Now we've got the King of Southern Bavaria!" one of them cried. So it was still the same. The workers might be united, but their leaders still quarreled among themselves. They were afraid that I, as President of the old Council, would prove dangerous to them, and it was only after long argument that I was released.

When I went back that evening to my lodgings the fat servant girl started back as if I'd been a ghost, and seized my hands to reassure herself.

"We thought you were dead," she explained. "A young man in a motor car stopped outside the house at lunch-time. Somebody cried out that it was you, and a whole crowd set on him and knocked him about and took him away unconscious. We had the Whites here in this very house until a few hours ago, but

they ran off when the Reds attacked. And they took
your ties with them. They haven't left one behind."

The pseudo Soviet which the Communists had denounced was finished, and now the "real" Soviet
began its work.

Scarcely a week had passed since the Communists
had declared that any Soviet was bound to fail, that
conditions were all against it, that the workers were
not ripe for it, that it would meet with disfavor in the
rest of Germany, that its formation would only be
a valuable service to the Reactionaries. But the victory of the workers on Palm Sunday had removed all
the Communists' scruples; that battle had united the
proletariat as nothing else had done; and so this "real"
Soviet was to be the creation of the masses, as the
pseudo Soviet had never been.

The Communists were in the thick of the fight.
Perhaps the new Soviet would be able to hold out
until Austria had also had a Communist revolution,
when they would be able to form a great Revolutionary *bloc* with Austria, Hungary and Bavaria.

Commissions were formed to reorganize the Red
Army, to suppress counter-revolutionary activities,
build up a proper economic fabric and regulate food-
supplies. The police were dismissed and the Red
Guard took over their duties, commanded by the
Communist, Eglhofer.

Eglhofer was one of the leaders of the naval mutiny
at Kiel in the autumn of 1918. One in every ten of

173

the sailors was sentenced to death, including Eglhofer, but the sentences were later commuted to penal
servitude for life. The November Revolution brought
freedom to them all. He lacked any organizing
capability, and chose his staff without the least dis-
crimination.

The first popular action of the new Government
was the confiscation of all hoarded foodstuffs; but
the confiscators kept it themselves. The moderate
newspapers were suppressed and the news sheet of
the Workers' and Soldiers' Councils became the Government organ. The factories were all closed down,
for a general strike of unspecified length had been
proclaimed.

Meanwhile Hoffmann's Government, which had
fled to Bamberg, had called the Bavarians to arms and
applied for military aid to the Reich Government at
Weimar, which sent two army corps to Northern
Bavaria. The Berlin newspapers printed atrocity reports from Munich stating that the station was in
ruins and that people were being rounded up in the
Ludwigstrasse to serve as living targets for the Red
Guard's rifle practice.

Actually Munich was quiet enough. The bark of
the Revolutionary Tribunal was a great deal worse
than its bite. Nobody was sentenced to death, nobody was shot, nobody was robbed or mishandled.

On April 15th Leviné was addressing a meeting
when his speech was interrupted by the ringing of

alarm bells. Nobody knew who had given the order, or what was behind it. Rumor had it that the citizens of Munich had organized a *Putsch*.

Alarm bells. Not the dull booming of great church bells, but the feverish jangling of hundreds of little bells, agitated and weak; a monotonous jangling, uncanny and menacing, that lashes the nerves, oppresses the heart, stirs the blood.

The watch outside the brewery slipped the safety catches of their rifles.

"Where's that row coming from?" I asked.

"From the Frauenkirche."

A year ago, when I had been arrested for complicity in the strike, I had refused to wear uniform or carry arms. I hated force and had vowed to suffer from force rather than employ it myself. Was I to break this vow now that Revolution had come? I had to break it. The workers had put their trust in me and made me their leader, and I was responsible to them. If I refused to defend them now, if I called on them to renounce force of arms, would I not be betraying that trust? If I stopped to think of the possible bloody consequences of everything I did I should have to refuse all office.

"You're sure that the Whites are responsible for the alarm?"

"Yes, they have already occupied the station."

"Who'll volunteer to come with me?"

175

Seven workmen came forward.

We went down a quiet, narrow street and as we approached the Theatinerstrasse a burst of machine-gun fire swept it from the Marienplatz.

"Down you get!"

We crawled forward. A motor car came tearing down the Theatinerstrasse.

"Halt!" I shouted and fired a shot into the air.

The car pulled up with a jerk, and a stout man jumped out with his hands full of cigarettes.

"Don't shoot!" he cried. "These are Austrian cigarettes!"

My friends grinned delightedly and seven hands stretched out for the cigarettes.

"Who are you?"

"Excuse me, I'm only the Austrian Consul."

"You've just come from the Marienplatz?"

"Yes."

"Who was that shooting?"

"I don't know."

"Did you meet any Whites?"

"I saw nothing. Look here—do take these cigarettes, won't you? They're real Austrians."

"Can't you really tell us anything?"

"I know nothing at all. Only that I'm scared stiff. Be a good fellow, and take these cigarettes."

My friends seized on them joyfully.

"They're Austrians all right!"

"We're your allies," the Consul declared.

"Stout fellow!" answered my friends.

"Will you let me go now?"

"Right away!" cried one of my men, as he lit his cigarette.

We crept up to the Frauenkirche like so many Indians; its pineapple domes loomed out of the darkness. We knocked at the caretaker's door and a woman opened the window; then with a "Jesus!" hastily barred the shutters. We banged again on the door.

It opened at last and the woman appeared in her nightdress, trembling in the doorway.

"Where's the caretaker?"

A little old man, clad only in his nightshirt, appeared behind his wife.

"Have mercy on him, gentlemen; don't shoot him. He's got sciatica that bad!"

"Nobody wants to shoot your husband. Who told you to ring the alarm bells?"

"I never rang 'em."

"Who did then?"

"Honest I didn't. Nobody's rung them. Honest to God I haven't. Don't shoot me, sir. Don't shoot me."

I quieted him down.

"Well, can you tell me what those bells were, then?"

"I couldn't tell for sure, sir. I know all the bells in Munich inside out; better than I know my own kids, I do. When the wind's from the west you can hear the bells of St. Peter's. Like a girl laughing, they are. And them in the Ludwigskirche like a woman having her first child. And if the wind shifts . . ."

"All we want to know is what bells were ringing just now."

"That's hard to say, sir. The wind's a bit funny tonight, sir. The Paulskirche I should think, sir. But I couldn't say for certain."

"All right, get back to bed and don't catch cold."

"As if he hadn't got sciatica already!" snapped his wife, and slammed the door in our faces.

We went on. The Marienplatz was deserted. We made our way to the railway station. One of my men was a cripple who wielded a rifle in one hand and a crutch in the other. In the stillness of the night his crutch hammered out the rhythm of our stride.

At the station we came across a picket of our own men.

"Where are the Whites?"

"Occupying the Paulskirche."

Behind a pillar we found an abandoned machine gun which we lugged along to the Paulskirche. Fifty paces from the steps we set up the machine gun, and one of the men let fly at the tower in his excitement. The echoes came thundering back.

All around us people flung up their windows, and a deep voice grumbled out:

"A nice lot you are! Shooting at this time of night!"

We advanced on the church at the double. The

178

enemy did not show themselves. The bell was peacefully silent.

We roused the caretaker.

"Who told you to ring the alarm bells?"

"That's just what I'd like to know!"

One of my men seized hold of him.

"Out with it, nasty dog! You're in with the Whites!"

"Who's in with the Whites? How the hell am I to tell one color from another in the middle of the night? A chap called Sendling came and told me to ring the bells. That's all I know."

At the district headquarters of the Communist Party Sendling told us that the order came from the City Commandant. The Whites were marching on Munich, and the workmen were going out to meet them.

We stopped a lorry in the street and drove on with it. On the outskirts of the town we got down and asked at an inn where the Whites were. Nobody knew.

In the bar there were three men from a cavalry regiment swilling beer and grumbling at the quality. Their horses were tied up outside. One of them gave me his horse and the other two came on with me.

We rode through the peaceful countryside under a moonlit, starry April sky. Presently we heard voices and turned into the dark, sheltering woods; somebody was cursing Toller and Leviné, so we knew we were with friends.

179

We approached a country railway station and saw a man suddenly run into the office. Dismounting, we followed him quickly and found him at the telephone.

"Who are you 'phoning to?"

He would not answer, so I took the receiver from him.

"A patrol?" a voice at the other end was saying.

"A regiment," I answered.

"A regiment?"

"A division!"

Silence.

Then: "Who's speaking?" asked the voice.

"Me."

I heard the receiver being hung up.

"You've been 'phoning the Whites!" I shouted at the station master. He said nothing.

We had no time to lose; we must get on. But before riding away we cut the wires.

At Karlsfeld we came upon a column of Munich workers and soldiers who had spontaneously, without military leadership, forced the White troops advancing on Munich from the north to turn and run. Now that they had warded off the attack and had lost touch with the White troops the united purpose of the crowd was broken, and they were conferring aimlessly in separate groups.

We rode along the high road toward Dachau. Suddenly there was a scream of bullets and my horse shied.

"Back!" I shouted.

180

As I turned I saw a horse rear, and one of my friends fell mortally wounded. We could not bury him until the next morning. In one of his pockets we found a letter:

"Dear Mother, how are you? I am very well. I am sitting here in the inn waiting for the Whites to come, they are attacking Munich, I don't know what the next few hours will bring. I prefer an honorable death."

The most trusted of the Munich workers were gathered together in an inn at Karlsberg.

"Toller ought to take command!" one of them cried.

"Command of a battery?" I asked, thinking of my experiences with the artillery in the war.

"No, command of the army," said an old white-haired Krupp's worker.

I resisted, trying to make it clear that the commander of an army needs qualities in which I was quite lacking.

"All you've got to do is to wear a pretty hat. Besides, if you don't know how you'll soon learn. The chief point is that we all know you."

I did not know what to answer.

It was thus I became an army commander.

Among the workers I found several young officers who had served in the old Imperial army. Together we formed a General Staff; the workers were drafted into battalions and we took up positions before Dachau, which was occupied by the enemy.

"A General Staff is no good without maps of the country," said our Infantry Commander, a nineteen-year-old student.

"That's a fact, it isn't," agreed a brewery hand who had been a corporal in the war.

In the early dawn I went back to Munich with my Infantry to collect equipment from the War Ministry. The reactionary officers at the War Ministry had also realized that a General Staff must have maps, and had thoughtfully provided us with some.

We returned to Karlsfeld and discovered that re-enforcements had come out from Munich, five hundred workmen from one of the big factories, armed and divided into companies and platoons.

I received an order from Eglhofer, the War Minister:

"Dachau to be stormed and taken, under cover of preliminary artillery bombardment."

I hesitated to carry out this order, for the peasants and farmers round Dachau were on our side, and it was up to us to avoid all unnecessary destruction as well as conserve our energies.

We despatched an ultimatum to the Whites on the following conditions:

"Withdrawal of the White troops to the far side of the Danube. Release of all members of the Central Council arrested on April 13th. Raising of the blockade of Munich."

This last condition was occasioned by Hoffmann's troops having blockaded Munich on the second day

182

of the Soviet. The English blockade of Germany during the war had aroused great indignation; but now Hoffmann did not scruple to try to starve his own countrymen into submission.

The Whites sent a First Lieutenant and a member of a Soldiers' Council to parley with us.

"My friends," I said to the soldier, ignoring the officer, "you're fighting against friends. You're taking orders from men who in the past have done nothing but oppress you, from the very men you rose up against last November."

"What about you?" he answered. "You've made a nice mess of things in Munich with your murdering and looting!"

"Who says that?"

"That's what it says in the papers."

"Very well then, go to Munich and see for yourself. I'll give you a safe-conduct and nobody'll touch you. Go and see for yourself what liars the newspapers are."

The officer, beyond all patience, yelled at him:

"Don't answer! Don't say another word! Not another word!"

"Who the hell do you think you're talking to?"

The Lieutenant got up and stalked off; the soldier whispered in my ear:

"It's all right. We shan't fight."

Accompanied by two of our men the negotiators returned to Dachau. After a couple of hours we heard that Hoffmann's men had accepted our ultimatum except in one particular: the troops would withdraw to Pfaffenhofen; they refused to retire to the other side of the Danube.

At four o'clock that afternoon I was startled by the boom of heavy guns. Had the Whites gone back on their word? But it turned out to be one of our own batteries which had been ordered to fire by an unknown Soldiers' Councilor.

A little later one of our negotiators came back alone to report that the White Commander had threatened to shoot his companion to punish the Reds for their dishonorable behavior in violating the armistice.

As Commander of the Red army I was responsible for the lives of all my men, and I decided to drive over to Dachau personally to explain the unfortunate affair to the Whites.

When we came to our front line there were no men to be seen. We went on and came to the barricade which the Whites had put up across the main road to Dachau. It was completely wrecked. Suddenly a burst of machine gun and rifle fire sprayed viciously round my car.

"Go on!" I cried to the chauffeur.

I saw our men advancing in open formation.

"Who gave the order to attack?" I asked one of the company leaders.

"A runner brought it from headquarters."

It did not occur to me that this attack might be the work of an *agent provocateur*, but a little later I discovered that one of the Soldiers' Councilors, who

184

had thrown in his lot with the Whites when they first advanced on Munich, had given the order for bombardment and attack on his own initiative, in order to add to the confusion.

Meanwhile, what was I to do? To order retreat in the middle of the action was out of the question; the only thing to do was to carry on and make as good a job of it as possible.

I returned to Karlsberg, sent up reserves in support and myself took command of a detachment.

The enemy's fire increased.

My men wavered and demanded support from the artillery. But I refused to bring the heavy guns into it and went forward with a handful of volunteers. The others followed. We came up with the main body and stormed Dachau.

As the fight developed the workers from the Dachau munitions factory attacked the Whites from the rear. The women among them were even more determined than the men. They disarmed the troops and drove them out of the town. The White Commander escaped on a railway engine. Our negotiator who had already been sentenced to be shot, managed to get away in the general confusion.

We took five officers and thirty-six men prisoner, and occupied the town.

Was I "the victor of Dachau"? No, it was the workers and the soldiers of the Soviet who had achieved the victory, not their leader. Dropping all party differences, they had rushed to defend the Republic. They had not waited to be told what to do; they had found unity in action.

The Whites fell back on Pfaffenhofen. Eglhofer sent a telegram ordering me to hold a court-martial and have the officer prisoners shot. I tore up the order, believing that generosity to the conquered should be an axiom of revolutionary conduct.

The prisoners were allowed to wander about at will; they were treated just like our own men. They were no more than friends who had been misled; they would soon recognize the justice of our cause, and see that they had been deluded. They were allowed to decide for themselves whether they would stay with us or be sent home.

Not that civil war was not too often brutal: I knew that in Berlin the counter-Revolutionaries had murdered Red prisoners in cold blood; but we were fighting for a better world; we were demanding humanity, and we had to show humanity ourselves.

The prisoners who returned home lived to fight against us on another day.

We occupied the headquarters of the Whites, whose Staff in Dachau had been composed of ex-Imperial officers. The Imperial army had been run by authority and blind obedience; the Red army was to be founded on free will and understanding. We did not try to copy the old abhorred militarism. The Red soldiers were not to be treated as machines; the fact that they were fighting for a cause they under-

186

stood should be enough, and discipline must result directly from the individual will to revolution.

Alas, the German workmen had been too long accustomed to blind obedience; they wanted only to obey. They confused brutality with strength, bluster with leadership, suppression of freedom with discipline. They missed their accustomed atmosphere; they found their freedom chaos.

Men who had fought for the Monarchy for four long years of blind sacrifice, who had endured all the horrors of war and hunger and want, now that they were fighting for their own cause became discontented after a few days because the Red front was not so well organized as the Imperial barracks had been.

Some two thousand men had taken part in the attack on Dachau, and after three days half of them had made their way back to Munich. We were compelled to check this wholesale French-leave, and to enforce the old military discipline in order to keep our numbers up to scratch. We even had to prohibit the sale of alcohol in the public houses.

The instinct for freedom and voluntary action simply does not exist in Germany. It will take years to erase the imprint of the old militarism. The old Germany found its strength in the blind submission of her citizens to authority, as taught in schools and barracks and preached in the press. But the new Germany can only be built up by free men. Blind submission can produce nothing.

During the war the people had become utterly demoralized, both bourgeois and workers, and above all the children.

One evening my door was wrenched open and some soldiers clattered in bearing a young girl on a stretcher. Her breath came in shuddering gasps, her eyes were wide and staring and full of terror, her face distorted, her clothes crumpled and torn.

"We've brought her here for her own protection," one of the soldiers said.

"Protection?"

"Yes, we found her in the men's quarters."

"In this condition?"

"More than twenty men had been at her."

"Take her to the hospital. I'll come along too."

On the way I heard the whole story. First one had assaulted her; he had recommended her to another; a third already stood waiting, and the others followed in a mad rout of unrestrained bestiality.

I was deeply stirred by the fate of this wretched child.

This was war, naked and brutal. Wilhelm II had called war a bath of steel. The German professors had declared that it aroused the moral and ethical conscience of the people. Just as you like, gentlemen, so long as you don't declare that this particular happening proved the depravity of the Socialists. Your own heroes, if they cared to be honest, could cite a thousand similar episodes from the Great War alone.

188

On the way to the hospital we met a soldier with a second girl who had just been hunted out of the men's quarters in the same way. I wanted to take her along to the doctor too, but since she wanted to rest for a moment I left her in charge of a sentry. When I returned to fetch her the sentry had disappeared, taking the girl with him.

The defeat at Dachau had demoralized Hoffmann's Government, and it was up to us to push forward before the Whites had time to reorganize themselves. We were strong enough to push them into the Danube and out the other side and so put an end to the food-shortage in Munich. For another advance would mean the occupation of the Hollanderau, a district where the peasants were friendlily disposed toward us.

But the advance was forbidden by the General Staff in Munich. The Commanders on the Dachau front were Independents, and the Munich Committee did not trust them.

The Whites were occupying Augsburg, and our men were to drive them out again. This would mean evacuating the important front at Dachau, which seemed to me nothing less than madness. I tried in vain to explain the consequences to the General Staff, but they offered me a plan of campaign which reminded me of Dr. Lipp's fantastic telegrams. The Red army was to fall back on Munich and a cordon of some hundred and fifty men set to keep watch; the guards would be in telephonic communication with one another and with the War Ministry, and when the enemy appeared the guard would communicate with the Ministry which would alarm the workers and the decisive battle would be fought outside the gates of Munich. This plan had been concocted by a gentleman named Hofer, who, after the collapse, turned out to have been a secret service agent in the pay of the White Command. It did not surprise us that this man had got on to the General Staff; it seemed the easiest thing in the world to gain the confidence of the military authorities. A young shopkeeper wanted to emigrate to Brazil. He went to see an acquaintance at the War Ministry, who asked him whether he had served in the war. Yes, he had been on the quartermaster's staff. Half an hour later he found himself entrusted with supreme command of the artillery.

The nights were becoming cold, and our men were only thinly clad. We needed a thousand overcoats, which were not to be had. I complained to the Executive Council about Herr Hofer's childish plan, about the military disorganization in Munich. In so doing I clashed with Leviné, so I turned to the Factory Councils.

I had no right to do so, but I believed that the salvation of the Revolution was more important than red tape.

The consequences of the General Strike were beginning to make themselves felt. There was no coal, no money, very little food. Until now the farmers had sent 150,000 liters of milk a day to Munich; now they were only sending 17,000 liters. A Governmental decree prohibited the making of milk into butter and cheese as a counter-Revolutionary action.

The grandiose economic schemes of the Socialists remained paper, as they always did throughout the German Revolution. Discontent among the workers was increasing every day. They had hoped that the Revolution would quickly better their positions. They were not content simply with power; they wanted immediate improvement in all the circumstances of their daily lives.

There was still no end to the internal strife among the Revolutionaries. Confusion increased and strength of purpose was dissipated in senseless cleavages.

Meanwhile Munich found itself surrounded by counter-Revolutionary troops. For a long time we had offered no resistance in Upper Bavaria, and now Bavarian, Württemberger and Prussian regiments were marching on Munich from every side. Isolated attacks by sections of the Red army could do little to stem the general advance.

Hoffmann's Government found it hard at first to find Bavarians who would march on Munich. The workers refused, and the soldiers were not to be relied on. Even the peasants were only half-hearted. But clever propaganda soon changed all that. Descriptions of the dreadful plans of the Munich Government were circulated; the peasants would find themselves robbed of their houses and their livestock; the citizens would find their savings confiscated and their family life broken up; priests would be murdered and monasteries looted. The effect of such propaganda was augmented by the promise of higher pay for the soldiers.

Hoffmann had to apply for help to the Reich. Soon the Generals were the real masters of the situation and Hoffmann's Government merely their tool.

An army of some hundred thousand men was advancing on Munich; we had only a few thousand at our disposal.

We had to decide whether we would fight to the finish or refuse battle. Whether we would retreat two paces so that, reorganized and strengthened, we might later advance one pace. We had no right to call the workers to battle when the only prospect was certain defeat; no right to call the workers to shed their blood for no purpose at all. So long as our opponents were kept in ignorance of our true weakness, so long as we could preserve at least the appearance of strength, it was our duty to save what little we could for the workers.

The Communists also knew perfectly well that our position was untenable, but they urged resistance, declaring that any compromise with Hoffmann would be treachery to the workers. They hoped by a spectacular military defeat to gain a great moral victory and new prestige, believing that defeat would rouse the proletariat to greater activity than ever. But the people had had enough of defeat. Misery and suffering and oppression are only useful as revolutionary stimuli when they serve to convince men that they are suffering unnecessarily and that it is in their power to alter things for the better.

I resigned my command of the army, feeling that I could no longer be responsible for the foolishness of the Executive Council and the General Staff. The Factory Councils knew nothing of the true state of affairs, and I dared not keep silent any longer.

At a meeting of the Factory Councils on April 26th, the internal disagreements came to a head and resulted in open schism. The Factory Councils passed a vote of censure on the Government and formed a Government of their own. But the Communists ordered the workers not to recognize this new Government, and the Communist Guard at the Wittelsbach Palace refused to lend its protection.

Thus two separate Governments were operating at once in Munich. The struggle between the opposing Revolutionary factions increased in fury from hour to hour.

The negotiations with Hoffmann's Government at Bamberg came to nothing; the Generals who were now firmly in the saddle wanted no understanding. They hated Bavaria, for it was the only place where the Republic was still a fact; in Bavaria alone the workers were still trying to save the November Rev-

193

olution. The overthrow of the Bavarian Soviet would mean the final defeat of the whole German Republic.

On April 30th the streets were empty and deserted. Occasional individuals still crept furtively in or out of their houses; little detachments of Red Guards and armed workers still paraded the town; the Red Flag still fluttered from the roof of the War Ministry and the Wittelsbach Palace; alarm bells were still jangling from the church towers, scaring frightened women from the streets and market-places. Only the children found any pleasure in all this; they delighted in the military cars tearing through the streets, and, imitating the grown-ups, played at being Revolutionaries, fought and conquered the enemy, captured towns and took prisoners, crying shrilly all the while: "Hurrah for the Reds!" or "Down with the Whites!" They arrested counter-Revolutionaries and triumphantly locked them up in sheds and cellars. It was terrible to watch this childish play; but still more terrible was the reality.

In the last few days the Red Guard had been making frequent and indiscriminate arrests and we had to liberate their prisoners. I rang up the prisons; there should be no repetition of the acts of desperation which had characterized the Paris Communes if I could help it.

The men who had been sent to parley with Hoffmann came back with the news that the Generals demanded the unconditional surrender of the town and of all the Revolutionary leaders. They knew perfectly well that the Factory Councils could not accept such terms.

Meanwhile, internal strife among the Revolutionaries had reached such a pitch that many of them dared not sleep in their own beds. Everybody distrusted everybody else; each saw an enemy in his neighbor.

Somebody brought me a pass and advised me to escape while I could. I tore up the pass.

Until the last minute I had hoped that any real bloodshed would be avoided; but now there was no question about it. The Government was forcing the battle on us.

We were all completely at sea. We all made mistakes, we all deserved blame, we were all inadequate—Communists just as much as Independents. Our gamble had been in vain, our sacrifices futile; but the workers had trusted us. How could we answer for ourselves to them now?

In my despair I hurried to Eglhofer at the War Ministry to get permission to return to Dachau as an ordinary soldier.

All night long, with hollow cheeks and burning, sleepless eyes, Eglhofer sat in his room. Soldiers came and went. Disaster was following on disaster.

"Augsburg taken by the Whites."

"The Red army breaking up."

"Civilians everywhere forming themselves into armed detachments."

"In the villages the Red Guards are being disarmed by the peasants and shot."

Eglhofer received the proffered reports without a word. Without a word he stamped my pass.

I left the War Ministry and hurried down the street. Suddenly I heard someone calling "Toller! Toller!"

I turned and saw Eglhofer at the window. He beckoned urgently, and I ran back to his room.

"You can't get through to Dachau. Our men are already retreating. The Whites are at Karlsfeld. All the outposts of the Red army have been broken. All this has just come through."

We stared at each other in silent consternation. Suddenly a soldier rushed in.

"The Whites have seized the railway station!" he shouted. Then he rushed off and yelled the same message into the next room. All down the corridor we heard him yelling:

"The Whites have seized the railway station! The Whites have seized the railway station!"

Before we could pull ourselves together the building was empty. One man only, Eglhofer's Adjutant, a young sailor barely twenty years old, came in and stood by his chief. Eglhofer took up his cap, stuck a revolver into his pocket and seized a couple of hand grenades which lay on the table before him.

"What are you going to do?" I asked.

"Stay here."

The young Adjutant spoke in his gentle, sober voice:

"I shall stay with you, Rudolf."

The telephone rang, and Eglhofer answered it. Then he turned to us.

"False alarm," he said. "The Whites aren't here yet."

Eglhofer's enemies have called him bloodthirsty, but actually he was a man of great sensibility hardened and rendered cruel by the treatment he underwent during the Kiel Mutiny.

That evening the Factory Councils sat for the last time, impotent in face of their fate. Their power was no more; the workers were overthrown, the Red army in confusion. They ordered the people of Munich to lay down their arms and allow the Whites unimpeded entry into the city. The Revolution was defeated.

Suddenly a man leaped onto the platform and shouted that nine prisoners had been shot in the high school building, nine civilians. The assembly was horror-struck. Quietly the workers dispersed; they knew that tomorrow they too would probably be stood against the wall and shot. The consequences of this lunatic act were terrible to think of; hundreds of our own men might be called upon to pay for it.

I tore to the high school and found it already abandoned by the garrison; only a few youths remained, and two Russian prisoners of war who had gone over to the Red army. I advised the boys to make themselves scarce and the Russians to get rid of their uniforms and hide. But the Russians were not helped by civilian clothes; a few days later they were outlawed, easy game for any drunken peasant with a gun. More than twenty Russians were killed in a single suburb of Munich. Bravely and quietly they had served as soldiers of the Revolution, and just as bravely, just as quietly, they faced the rifles of the firing party.

Behind a locked door in the school I heard cries.

"Where is the key?"

Nobody knew.

We rattled on the door, but it did not give so we drove it in.

The moans and cries became shriller and ghastly to hear; then suddenly all was still. The door gave in and before us in the far corner of the room cowered six people in the fear of death.

When we explained that we had come to release them, not to shoot them, they could hardly believe their ears.

And who were these poor creatures? Not ringleaders of the counter-Revolution. Not big game at all; simply half a dozen unfortunate wretches, including an old outside porter who had torn down a Revolutionary poster to keep the rain off his barrow, an innkeeper who had been denounced by a waiter he had dismissed, a discontented workman.

A soldier took me to the shed where the bodies lay.

198

They were not White hostages, as the papers afterwards declared, but civilian suspects. When the
news came through that the Whites would shoot
down every captured Red without mercy, the local
Commandant ordered these suspects to be shot without referring to any responsible official. There was
a woman among the dead, a Jewish painter. I lit a
match and stared at the ghastly sight in the dim,
flickering light.

The soldier told me how they had died, standing
erect and fearless. One of them lit a cigarette and
met his death as he smoked.

With the same bravery were our own men to die
on the morrow.

As I stood looking down at these corpses I thought
of the war, of the witches' cauldron of the Bois-le-
Prêtre, of the countless millions murdered throughout
the length and breadth of Europe.

When would man cease from this endless harrying,
torturing, murdering, and martyrizing of his fellows?

In an adjoining shed a light was burning and there
was our Dachau paymaster sitting amidst a confusion
of provision sacks and chests at work on his ledgers.

"I'm bringing the accounts up to date," he explained. "The Whites shan't have a chance to say
that we didn't keep our books in order if I can help it.
There's fifty pfennigs I can't trace. Don't disturb
me."

He went on counting.

There he sat, good-humored and unsuspecting,

199

adding up figures and assessing stocks so that everything should be in order when he is led out to be shot.

"If the Whites find you here they'll put you up against the wall."

"Will you take the responsibility if I go?"

"I will."

He looked sadly at the incomplete account, and at the door suddenly turned and hurried back to the table, ruled a line under the last column of figures and wrote: "Fifty pfennigs not accounted for." Then he went.

My great care now was to get the bodies out of the place if I could before daylight. The very sight of them would be enough to lash the Whites into an orgiastic frenzy of revenge. I went to the surgical clinic and begged the doctor on duty to have the corpses fetched at once.

It was not done.

Next day, after the victory of the Whites, placards and newspapers screamed out the tale of the mutilated corpses which had been found with their sexual organs hacked off and thrown into dustbins. Actually the relics in the dustbin came from slaughtered pigs, and there had been no mutilations at all, but by the time the truth was published the damage had been done. Hundreds of wretched innocents paid for that imaginary atrocity with torture and death.

In the dawn of the first of May I walked through the quiet streets, anywhere, nowhere. I met some soldiers who told me of the collapse of the Red front. One of them had a copy of *The Red Flag*.

"The Communists are calling on us to defend Munich," he said. "Why can't they organize the defense, then?"

I remembered a girl I had known very well in my University days and decided to go to her flat and beg a few hours' sleep.

There I flung myself fully dressed on the bed, and thought wearily to myself: "Today is the first of May. . . ."

12. Flight and Arrest

The Whites entered Schwabing in close formation, and the people cheered at their open windows and showered the troops with presents. One poorly dressed woman ran up to an officer and gave him a rose. A group of soldiers posted themselves in front of the church, just opposite our house.

The first of May.

I was standing at the window when my friend came in and caught my hand.

"They're watching us. When I came upstairs just now somebody opened the door of the third floor flat. They must have seen you, and been suspicious."

"I've got a friend, Dr. Berut, who lives just round the corner," I said.

"I'll fetch him."

In a very few minutes Dr. Berut arrived.

"You must get away," he said. "They have already shot one man on the strength of a vague resemblance to you. The people don't realize that you wanted to rescue the prisoners; they regard you as one of the murderers."

"Where shall I go?"

"Come with me. You can't stay here; this place belongs to a foreigner, and they're sure to have it searched."

I put on my overcoat and turned the collar up; as we went downstairs the front door of the third floor flat opened.

"Don't stop!" Berut warned me in a low voice.

Two officers were standing at the street door.

"I'll go first," said Berut. "You follow me."

One of the officers glanced at me suspiciously. I went up to him and said:

"Prussian or Bavarian?"

"Bavarian, of course!" he snapped in a strong Prussian accent.

I wished him good day; he reciprocated; and I went on.

Aeroplanes were circling over the town dropping leaflets; but I dared not pick one up.

Berut was waiting for me at his door. Beside him the hall porter's wife was reading one of the leaflets.

"I'd make a nice pile for myself, I would, if I knew where them fellers Toller and Leviné have hid themselves!"

"Do you really want the money so much?"

"Well, a bit of cash does no one any harm, sir."

I went quickly upstairs to Berut's flat.

In the distance there was a dull roll of heavy artillery.

So they were fighting after all.

"The Reds are holding the Stachusplatz; the Whites have surrounded it."

"I must get out there somehow."

"You'd never get through. You'd be recognized and shot. How do you think you'd get past the cordon?"

Berut went out; after a time he came back with a stranger.

"I'm no friend of yours," said this stranger. "I'm not even a Socialist; but they want to kill you, and I'll help you. If you come to my flat you can stay there until it's safe to go elsewhere."

"How do you know they won't search your flat?"

Berut laughed.

"His father is a Bavarian duke who's cleared out because of us. If you're safe anywhere it will be there."

I waited until dusk and then made my way to this unknown friend's flat. Such men are somehow always there when help is needed.

"I'll tell the cook you're a friend from Berlin, and that you're ill and can't leave for a day or two."

Berut came to see me next day and greeted me with a broad grin:

"I see your corpse is on view in the mortuary."

"My corpse?"

"Here's a paper with the official report. You were shot and taken to the mortuary. The police got hold of the chauffeur who drove you to Dachau and he

204

identified your corpse and wept with emotion. You've nothing to fear for the next day or two; they won't be looking for you."

I read the report of my death and thought of my mother. She, too, had read the news, and for three days she sat crouched on a low stool, surrounded by shrouded mirrors, and mourned her son. On the fourth day she learned that I was still alive.

The only person to visit me in my hiding place was Berut. The police too had learned by now that I was still alive, and one day Berut didn't come; he had been arrested. At police headquarters a detective put a revolver to his head and threatened to blow his brains out if he didn't reveal my hiding place. Berut led him to the wrong house, then admitted he had made a mistake, but said he could not remember where I was now. An officer saved him from being shot.

Meanwhile the Government had set a price upon my head, and on all the hoardings a placard was stuck up:

10,000 MARKS REWARD
HIGH TREASON!

In accordance with Paragraph 81 of the German Criminal Code a warrant has been issued for the arrest of Ernst Toller, student of law and philosophy, here depicted. He was born on the 1st of December, 1893, at Samotschin in Posen, in the Government district of Bromberg, in the Parish of Mar-

*gounin, son of the shopkeeper Max Toller and his
wife Ida, née Kohn.*

*Toller is of slight build, height about 5 foot 6 or
7; has a thin, pale face, clean shaven; large brown
eyes, sharp glance, closes his eyes when thinking;
has dark, almost black, wavy hair; speaks cultured
German.*

*For his capture, or for information leading to his
capture,*

TEN THOUSAND MARKS
reward is offered.

*Relevant information should be lodged with the
public prosecutor, Munich, or with the Chief Inspector of the Munich C.I.D.*

*To facilitate the search please telegraph news of
apprehension and spread this description as exten-
sively as possible.*

*In case of capture abroad an extradition order will
be applied for.*

Munich, 13th May, 1919.

The picture on the poster was poor, and I had
grown a mustache since it had been taken; but I was
apprehensive about the cook; she might easily recognize me, and I decided it was high time to find another
hiding place.

But no one would take me in. The intellectuals
were scared, and the homes of the workers were
thoroughly searched every day.

One morning I was awakened by the echoing
tread of soldiers on the march. I ran to the window

206

in time to see a patrol come to a halt in front of the house.

So that's that, I thought.

My unknown host was at his wit's end. "We'll both be shot," he said.

Pointing to the curtain pole he added: "That's hollow and full of ammunition—and there are pistols. My people hid them when the Reds ordered everyone to give up their fire-arms."

He put on his spectacles; took them off and polished them; looked at me perplexedly with his short-sighted eyes.

"We must do something about it," I said. "Have you any decent clothes?"

"I've got a cutaway, yes."

"Put it on, then. Have you a monocle?"

He pulled out a drawer. "Here's a whole collection of my father's."

"Stick one in your eye."

He stared at me open-mouthed.

"These things may do the trick," I said. "There's not an officer in the army who wouldn't click his heels when confronted with a monocle and cutaway."

My idea was perfectly idiotic—what earthly good would it be for a man to open his front door at six o'clock in the morning attired for a fashionable race-meeting? But at the moment it seemed to me a heaven-sent inspiration. I helped my friend dress, selecting a suitable tie with great care, and when we had finished he really looked the picture of innocent prosperity.

While this comedy was being enacted the soldiers were searching the other flats. They began with the attic, which belonged to a painter, a well-known Nationalist. Before he could collect his wits he was sent flying by a box on the ear.

"Artist?" yelled the Sergeant. "Artist my eye!"

Above our heads we could hear heavy footsteps; they were searching the first floor flat now. At any moment they would be knocking at our door.

Then from below we heard an uproar and the porter's wife weeping and wailing. They had arrested her husband and dragged him out into the street.

We waited. We exchanged fatuous remarks and stared at the door. A bell rang, and we rushed out into the corridor. But it wasn't our bell. We were stiff with suspense, and neither of us could utter a word. They must be coming now. If only they would come and get it over! The seconds dragged out to intolerable lengths.

Suddenly I heard a command in the street below. I ran to the window and looked out, and could scarcely believe my eyes, for the soldiers were being formed up and marched off with the unhappy porter staggering in their midst with his hands up.

Were they as sure of us as all that? Had they put sentries at the door?

Nobody came.

Later we heard that the officer, reading the exalted name on the name-plate, had called his men off.

The German Revolution knew whom to respect.

My future looked a little brighter, but there was still no time to lose; go I must. But where?

Shootings, man-handlings and arrests had intimidated even the bravest; but at last that evening a young woman volunteered to hide me for the night in her parents' flat.

In front of her house, when we arrived, were some soldiers flirting with the house-maid. I hesitated, but there was no going back now; and unrecognized I pushed past them into the house.

The girl's father was a doctor; his living quarters were on one side of the house, his consulting room and his daughter's room on the other. It was imperative he should notice nothing; he would not have hesitated to give me away.

Weary with the day's excitement I stretched myself out on the sofa in the little living room and fell asleep, and in my sleep I seemed to hear the girl's voice saying:

"The door has just been unlocked."

"Somebody's just knocked."

"Some people are coming."

I roused myself and listened but could hear nothing. I looked at the clock. It was half past five!

The girl was standing by my sofa.

"The maid will be here in a minute to tidy up the room. You must hide."

I crouched down on the floor of her bedroom, hidden under a pile of linen and blankets, scarcely able to breathe. I dared not stir, for the maid could see the bedroom reflected in the mirror in the living room.

At last she went.

"My father will come in any moment now to say good morning. You'd better go into the bathroom. Hide in the bath and cover yourself up with the bath-sheet."

I crouched in the chilly bath and listened; I heard footsteps, heard the door being opened; waited; heard footsteps once again, this time retreating. I slunk back into the living room.

"My father hasn't noticed anything, but you can't stay here another night."

"Do you know anybody who would take me in?"

"Why not Rainer Maria Rilke? I'll ask him."

Rilke himself came to see me that afternoon.

When I saw him I thought of a picture that I had seen in some book—a Tartar, loaded with booty, riding wearily on his little mongol pony through the brazen desert. He brought my friend a bunch of long-stemmed tea-roses, obviously chosen with great care; neither bud nor full-blown, they seemed to hesitate delicately between furling their silken petals up again and spreading them wide to catch the air.

He regarded me sadly and watchfully with those pale gray, heavily lidded eyes; then his eyes dropped and he rested his chin with its drooping mustache on his hands, gloved as usual.

"I am greatly troubled, but I am afraid you wouldn't be safe with me. My house has been searched twice already. The Soviets took my house under their protection but I forgot to tear down their notice on the door, and now of course the Whites have got their eye on me. The police came again only two days ago, and among my photographs they found a picture of you. So that of course served as a pretext for further persecution."

So Rilke left; soon afterwards he was expelled from Munich. He was not interested in political struggles; but because he was a poet the police regarded him with suspicion.

In the end I found a man prepared to take me in— the artist Lech. I could not afford to hang about any longer, but how was I to get to him? The poster demanding my capture covered all the hoardings and my face was only too well known. But with the help of the actor, Werin, I disguised myself. I wrapped myself in a heavy overcoat and powdered my eyebrows and hair; a few minutes later an elegant old gentleman, an obvious spinal patient, left the house, his back a little bent.

Lech lived in a house in Schwabing with a big garden. I stayed with him three weeks. All day long I had to cross the room bent double so that nobody should see me through the window, and only at dusk could I venture out for a few minutes in the garden to fill my lungs with the spring air. Lech and his wife had by no means too much to eat, but the little they had they generously shared with me. The days passed emptily. I read in the papers that the police were still looking for me, and that there was scarcely a town in which I had not been seen. Trains were held up, villages surrounded. Once they even carried the search into Austria, and soldiers searched Schloss Ottensheim on the Danube where some relations of mine lived. The Swiss police on the border arrested a doctor who was alleged to have smuggled me across. My brother, living in Eastern Germany, was also threatened.

The poster by now had penetrated to even the smallest hamlets all over Germany, and workers and their wives tried to help me by defacing my portrait from it.

They also looked for me in the studio of another painter, Sohn Rethel, who had to go round with them with his hands up while they searched; when they didn't find me they took it out of him in general rough handling.

Police, soldiers, informers, all were after those ten thousand marks.

Two detectives entered a flat in the Romerstrasse. While they were searching the rooms the bell rang. Very gently and cautiously one of the detectives opened the door and found himself face to face with soldiers from Hoffmann's army.

"That's Toller!" their officer cried.

A shot rang out and the detective dropped.

I knew from the newspapers what sort of a reception awaited me if I was captured; yet I was still unwilling to leave the town. I dyed my hair with peroxide, and after a few dips it turned red. I scarcely knew myself in the mirror.

A hidden door, papered over, led from the studio to a built-out bay. We hung the door with pictures, and only one friend knew of my hiding place.

One evening a woman came to see me, who said she had helped others to escape and would get me out of Munich. She persuaded us to show her over the flat, to show her the studio and the hidden recess behind the secret door.

At four o'clock next morning there was a pummeling on the front door. The police! I jumped out of bed, ran to the window and saw that the house was surrounded by soldiers.

"They're here," I called to my friends in the next room. "One of you get into my bed at once."

I slipped into my hiding place in my shirt, barred the door from the inside, and waited.

I heard approaching footsteps; then voices. Somebody was tapping on the wall to sound it. The knocking came nearer and nearer. The seconds dragged endlessly. Then they were actually knocking on my hidden door. Now they couldn't help finding me. I held my breath. But the knocking continued and gradually receded. After a few minutes there was silence.

They had not found me. How extraordinary! But I was not glad; I knew they would find me soon enough. If only they'd shoot me outright and not torture me as they tortured Landauer, Eglhofer, and so many others.

Outside Lech called softly:

"Stay where you are!"

Then the searchers came into the room again. I heard a flat voice:

"Where is the paper-covered door corresponding to the one on the floor above?"

Another voice shouted:

"There!"

Down came the pictures, and through cracks in the door came slits of light. I pushed the door open and faced detectives and soldiers.

"You're looking for Toller. Well, here he is."

"Put up your hands!" one of them shouted.

The detectives looked at me sharply; they hardly recognized me. One soldier knelt down and pointed his gun at me with goggling eyes and a finger that fumbled on the trigger.

"You are—?"

"Yes, I'm Toller. I shan't try to escape. If you shoot me now it won't be while attempting to escape. You can all bear witness to that."

The police fell on me and snapped the handcuffs on.

214

"Gentlemen, am I to go with you in my shirt?"

They took off the handcuffs to let me dress.

As I was led past my hosts I tried to prevent them being incriminated by saying:

"These people had no idea who I was."

But it was no good. Lech got many months' imprisonment.

We went through the streets, empty in the cold light of dawn. Three soldiers headed the little procession; I followed, handcuffed to a policeman on either side; three armed soldiers brought up the rear.

In the Luipoldstrasse a clock struck five. An old woman was hobbling along to Mass, and at the church door she turned and saw me.

"Have you got him?" she cried. Then she dropped her eyes and told her beads with trembling fingers. Suddenly from the open church-door the wrinkled mouth screeched:

"Kill him!"

13. A Cell, a Prison Yard, a Wall

In the corridor in front of my cell two soldiers were posted with fixed bayonets. News of my capture had spread through the building like wildfire, and faces peered through the bars from every cell. Hands waved to me, old friends welcomed me, even the street walkers denied their profession with shouts of "We're all political prisoners here!" and "Three cheers for the Soviet!"

The police officials filed past my cell in a long procession. Again and again the shutter over the spyhole slid back and an eye goggled at me. The human eye can look very cruel; the pupil stares curiously out of its surrounding white. I turned my back on the door.

The door of the cell was unlocked and two men tramped in: Police Inspector Lang and a blacksmith.

"What chains do you want?" asked the blacksmith.

"Same as Leviné," answered the Inspector.

The blacksmith took a great heavy chain, riveted one end to my left wrist and the other to my ankle.

I laughed.

"You'll soon be laughing on the wrong side of your face!"

"Not unless you can chain my thoughts too."

The door clanged behind them. I felt strangely carefree and cheerful. The strain of the last few weeks was over; I need not slink about any more, bent double. Once more I could stretch myself to my full height and walk about my cell free and unrestrained.

I was taken to be photographed. I had to sit on a chair with my prison number on it while the photographer jammed a traveling cap on my head and photographed me from every angle. The picture was afterwards published in the papers with retouched swollen lips and protruding "criminal eyes" calculated to strike horror into the stoutest heart.

"If they're any good I'd like one or two," I said.

Over the tall stiff collar came the answer, spat out: "Before they're finished you'll be meal for worms."

When they came to take my fingerprints I protested. I was not a criminal.

"You shut up, you swine! You filthy blackguard! None of your lip!"

And he seized my hand and smeared it in the dye and took the prints.

I was taken to the examination room. Lieberich, the public prosecutor, was sitting at the table; a small, thin little man with a wrinkled, deeply lined face. His lackluster eyes were surrounded by a network of crow's-feet; his lips were thin and sharp.

"Where's your guard?" he shouted.

Soldiers with fixed bayonets appeared and took up position on either side of my chair.

"Must I wear my chains here?" I asked.

Short and sharp came the answer: "Yes, you must. You will give evidence against Leviné?"

"Against Leviné? Leviné had nothing to do with shooting the prisoners."

"You fought against him in the Soviet Republic?"

"Yes, but this side of the barricades."

Lieberich's voice became oily.

"Herr Toller, you have the chance now of doing yourself a good turn."

"Will you please have my statement taken down?"

"Just as you like. What is your religion?"

"I have none."

He turned to a stenographer:

"Put down 'Jew, non-professing.' . . . So you want to defend these murders?"

"What murders? Who shot Gustav Landauer? Who put to death innumerable innocent people?"

"I object to your tone. Gustav Landauer was a rebel. He was legally and properly tried."

The questioning went on for hours. Herr Lieberich took short notes from which he dictated a statement which occasionally reproduced my own words but more often distorted them out of all recognition.

After the examination I asked for permission to read the newspapers.

"For your nerves' sake I cannot grant such permission. Take care of yourself, and don't over-excite yourself. . . . Take him away!"

That night I woke up in my cell to find someone bending over me with one of my despatches to the Red army.

"Is this your signature here?"

"Let me sleep," I answered.

"I don't mean you any harm, really; will you have a cigarette?"

"I want to sleep."

And I turned my face to the wall and was silent.

The shutter over the peep-hole was pushed back; outside stood the two sentries, workmen from Stuttgart. We talked together like old comrades about the war and the Revolution; I forgot I was a prisoner and they forgot they were warders.

One of the men brought me a little butter; two hours later he was punished by dismissal. But that night the shutter was drawn again and somebody pushed a newspaper through.

"Leviné shot," I read.

My heart beat hard. This was murder, pure and simple, and the Social Democrats had done nothing to stop it. The War Minister who had pledged his loyalty to the Soviet Republic had withheld his vote when the question of pardon was being considered. The fact that the Social Democrats had not prevented this murder showed how impotent they were, how weak, how degenerate—yet their millions of supporters had not uttered a word of protest.

The charge on which he had been sentenced to death was infamous to the last degree. When Leviné joined the Soviet it had already been in existence for a week and the alleged High Treason already committed. Leviné's action was, legally speaking, merely the aiding and abetting of High Treason; a crime punishable by imprisonment, not by death. Leviné, however, was condemned to death and executed. The eager judges knew what they were doing. The "first" Soviet Republic, they said, was only a revolt; it was not until Leviné appeared that High Treason was committed. They bespattered his honor and condemned him to death. And only yesterday these same judges had found men who had only assisted in the "revolt" guilty of High Treason, and sentenced them to long terms of imprisonment.

And then they wondered why the people had lost all faith in the Courts. So short were their memories that they waxed righteously indignant when accused of judicial corruption.

Munich was entirely under the thumb of the old ruling classes. They defended the Republic; they, who had persecuted Pacifists and Socialists in the name of the Monarchy, now persecuted Revolutionaries in the name of the Republic. A few years later they would be turning against the men who now employed them.

After some days I was transferred to Stadelheim prison. I sat handcuffed between two detectives in the car; opposite me sat an officer with his revolver in his hand; we were escorted by a lorry of soldiers with machine guns.

As we passed down the Maximilianstrasse I saw how the whole face of the town had changed in the last weeks. Officers in uniform, monocled, exquisitely groomed, smothered with orders, flirted with smartly dressed women. The bourgeoisie was on top again. In the poorer quarters people glanced at our car with furtive interest. They had seen too many prisoners in the last few weeks.

We pulled up at the prison gates. Scrawled in chalk was the *Mene mene tekel* of the day:

"This is where we make sausages of Spartacists. Reds executed free of charge."

The garrison received us with jeers and hoots. A police inspector offered to help me carry my little box.

"That blighter doesn't want any help," a soldier yelled. "What he wants is shooting!"

In the search room I had to undress; they pawed me all over and took away my clothes, comb, matches, handkerchief, everything. I was taken to a cell, the lock grated behind me and I was swallowed up in the vast silence of the prison.

Apparently I was in a block of cells reserved for hardened criminals.

The walls were bleak, gray and bare. The frosted

glass window was high above my head, but when I opened it I could see a little strip of sky. The cell contained a folding table, a bench, a plank bed with ragged gray blankets, and in the corner a stinking chamber-pot.

In my old prison I had been able to feel the pulse of hundreds of other prisoners round me; I saw their faces; I heard their voices. And sometimes, at night, I heard the comforting roar of the city. Now I was terribly alone. In that cage of heavy silence I was overwhelmed by a sense of being utterly abandoned. I spoke out loud just to hear the sound of a human voice, but my words sounded hollow and lifeless; I broke off in the middle of a useless sentence.

I read the list of prison regulations; I hunted for the marks of other prisoners on the walls and found roughly scratched the names of men who had been incarcerated for years on end in this little room. In one corner I found some words scrawled half illegibly in pencil. I managed to make them out: "They're coming for me now to shoot me. I am innocent. May 2nd, 1919."

The spy-hole shutter slid softly back and a young warder in army uniform looked through.

"Comrade. . . ."

I ran to the door. I was not alone!

"I was in the Red army; but when the Whites took the town we pulled off our red armlets. You are in Leviné's cell."

The shutter slid back into place. So Eugen Leviné

had slept in this cell before he was put against the wall. And over there, in the women's prison, his wife lay moaning, pressing her hands to her ears to shut out the sound of the shot which killed him.

Suddenly the building was alive with echoing footsteps. The bolts of the cell screeched, the little service hatch was flung open and my midday meal arrived: a lump of rank American bacon and pickled cabbage.

"Who is in the next cell?" I asked.

"A murderer awaiting execution."

"And on the other side?"

"A lifer."

"Where are the other political prisoners?"

"Over there, in the other block."

In the night I was awakened by the rattle of machine-gun fire. What did that mean? A new struggle? Would I be released? The shooting died down; started up again; isolated shots rang out; bullets spattered on the brickwork. In the morning the warder told me there was always shooting at night; the soldiers did it for amusement; he had got used to it. He warned me not to show myself at the window.

Leviné's execution had created a great sensation. The general impression seemed to be that I would go the same way. In all countries "solidarity" was the catchword of the moment.

On the second day at Stadelheim I was taken into the yard for exercise. I walked round and round

223

the little square entirely alone, watched by two warders. Soldiers hung out of the windows and jeered.

I felt the shadows of dead friends round me. I saw the wall against which some thirty-six men had been shot. It was pitted with countless bullet-holes, spattered with lumps of dried flesh, shreds of human brains, blood-stained hairs.

The earth at the foot of the wall was stained with blood. I counted the marks on the wall and the warder told me why they were so low; the drunken Württemberger soldiers aimed at the stomach and knees. "You're too good to be killed outright," they would say. "We'll give you one in the belly to go on with."

I stood, very cold, looking at the wall.

This was where they had shot a boy who brought up ammunition to the Red Guards.

This was where a woman died who hid a hand-grenade in her bosom to save her lover.

This was where Leviné fell dead, crying, "Long live the World Revolution!"

A little door divided us from the courtyard of the women's prison, where Gustav Landauer was shot.

A young man with a chubby, friendly, almost child-like face crossed the courtyard. "That's Eisner's murderer, Graf Arco," said the warder.

So this smiling boy was Eisner's murderer. To this child's folly could be traced the attempt on Auer's life and the consequent confusion, the rise of the

Soviet Republic, then its downfall and the triumph of the Whites.

I could not sleep; I heard a voice wailing:
"I am not guilty. I am not guilty."
Toward morning it ceased.

While I was taking my exercise two women crossed the yard, a girl supported by an old woman. The old woman was silent, her lips tightly shut. The girl cried without ceasing:

"My husband, my husband, I want my husband!"

A warder led the women to a little shed in the corner of the courtyard where were several roughly fashioned coffins. I counted them every day.

The girl threw herself onto one of the coffins and collapsed.

"I want my husband," she wailed, "give me back my husband." Suddenly she jumped up. "What an ugly coffin you've given him!" she cried.

One day I was taken down to an officer for further cross-examination. In the ground-floor corridor I noticed six men in uniform, obviously students and ex-officers.

"That's he!" one of them said.

After the examination the warder took me upstairs again; the six soldiers were still standing in the corridor, and followed on our heels muttering among themselves.

"You red scoundrel, you filthy Spartacist swine!

You wait. We've got a bullet with your name on it. Your number's up this time!"

The warder unlocked the door leading back to my block of cells; I passed through, and the door was shut in their faces.

An hour later the young warder spoke to me through the food hatch:

"Herr Toller, don't take your exercise today. I heard what those men were saying; they think it's a good opportunity to do you in. One of them is going to kick out at you in the yard, and when you stumble forward the others will shoot and declare that you were 'shot while attempting to escape.'"

Soon I was called to exercise.

The six men were still lurking by the door. We went downstairs and they followed silently. For a few moments I felt afraid; I had so often read of men "shot while attempting to escape." Then I became quite calm. I noticed trivial details. I saw that a chunk of mortar had fallen out between two bricks. I noticed the warder's grubby collar and a large red pimple behind his left ear.

We had arrived at the iron door to the ground-floor cells, and from there a side door led to the courtyard. The old warder, Müller, must have known of the plot against me, but did not dare warn me. He had to take me out into the yard as regulations demanded. But at the iron door to the cells he disobeyed regulations. He unlocked it, pushed me through, followed quickly himself, locked the door from the inside and so saved my life.

I reported the incident to the Governor of the prison. A few weeks later he had me up before him; the chief warder had corroborated my story, but they had been unable to establish which men were on duty on the day in question. All inquiries as to the identity of the six men remained fruitless.

I fell ill, and an operation became necessary. I was taken to a surgical clinic and isolated in a special room for prisoners; the window was barred—even when you are severely ill you might try to escape! Two armed soldiers stood guard at the door, and detectives hovered in an adjoining room.

During the first sleepless night after the operation I was tortured by thirst and rang for a glass of water.

A young nun opened the door cautiously, paused at the holy water stoup and crossed herself.

"Water, please," I said.

She hurried out and soon returned with a glass, but her hand shook, her face was pale; she advanced hesitatingly with wide and frightened eyes.

"May I make the sign of the cross over you?" she whispered.

I stared at her in surprise.

"All the sisters say that you are the Devil."

I laughed, which hurt me, and she blushed and hastily set the glass down.

"Please do let me," she pleaded. She made the

227

sign of the cross over my bed, let me drink, and then vanished.

She came again the next night without my having rung. And after that she came every night. She got over her terror, and sitting by my bedside she told me confidingly all about her home village in Upper Bavaria, about her brother who owned a farm, and what a poor livelihood he made out of it, how all his work hardly brought in enough to live on and he had their mother to support as well, how the cow gave very little milk and the towns kept prices down. He had a horse too, a white one; in the old days she had fed him and groomed him herself, and as she went to and from the stable he would neigh to her. But now she would never go home again any more; she was the bride of Christ and had bidden the world farewell.

Once she asked me: "Do you believe in God?"

But she went on before I could answer, and her voice betrayed her fear of what my answer would be.

"Many people say they don't believe in God, and yet God dwells in their hearts."

On my last night in the clinic she bent over my bed and kissed me.

In the morning the prison van was already waiting when a Novice came in shyly and thrust a little parcel secretly into my hand.

"From Sister Ottmara; a little cross. It is very holy; a reliquary-cross. It will protect you always, all your life."

14. Court-Martial

The day before my trial the barber came to cut my hair, which by now was piebald. The ends, which were red, must be left, he said, for the Public Prosecutor wanted the judges, the press and the public to see for themselves to what lengths of deceit I had gone to avoid the arm of the law. "Cheer up, Herr Toller," he said, "you're quite in the fashion. Everybody has a bit of peroxide about them today."

In the morning I was taken by car to the Law Courts, escorted by a lorry full of armed soldiers. Two policemen took me into the Court, and I sat down on the chair provided. I saw nobody, neither press nor public, but only the great gilt-framed picture which hung over the judge's empty chair: Good King Ludwig, whom the people called *Millibauer*. I had last seen him during the war. I remembered his bent knees in their concertina trousers as he strode down the ranks of volunteers. Now he was living on an estate in Hungary, but his heroic portrait remained to preside over the Republic.

"Stand up for their worships!" the policeman said in my ear.

I grinned at *Millibauer*. Then the judges advanced in solemn file through the wide-flung doors: three sets of robes, two uniforms, and two immaculate frock-coats. Out of the clothes sprouted heads, and the heads had eyes; hard probing eyes and cold fishy ones; inquisitive shifty eyes and vacant steel-blue ones.

The little procession was curiously lacking in dignity, and I could not rid myself of the feeling that they were only playing at being judges, just as we used to play at being parsons and bandmasters when we were children.

Every day while I was there an old woman used to bring me a thermos bottle full of soup; something to warm me up, she would say. The learned judges, poring over the Imperial Book of Statutes, which was their Bible, decided that I was guilty of High Treason. They were certainly wiser than my old woman with the thermos bottle; they despised the workings of common sense, which should have told them that the laws of High Treason as set forth in their Statute Book were drawn up exclusively to preserve a Monarchy long since fallen.

It was just the same with the charge that I had actively conspired to overthrow the Constitution. The old Constitution had been overthrown by the very men who brought me before this Court, yet it had not been replaced by another. My old woman could have told them that, but the judges blandly ignored the position. What sort of justice, then, could one expect from such men—from the two officers in full-dress uniform and the dusty, dried-up little gentlemen in their black gowns, from the two "assessors" who were not concerned with the rights and wrongs of the case at all but merely with seeing that everything was carried out in accordance with the regulations?

These "assessors" were timid and apprehensive in face of a task which would have been beyond them had they been a hundred times cleverer. They sat wiping the sweat from their foreheads, only now and then allowing themselves ·the indulgence of a glance at their envious neighbors or proud wives sitting in the public gallery. If only it were all over.

Poor wretch in the dock!—torn from the peaceful monotony of your daily round and hauled up before the judges to answer for yourself; what of you? It will be proved to you that everything you ever did had a cause, was the logical and inevitable outcome of some previous action. You must confess to the motive; you may not know what it was, but you must confess to it. So many motives go to the making of even one action: curiosity, an emotion, a memory; perhaps even the sun itself, or a storm, a meal, a drink, a long-dead ancestor. When a lamp suddenly flickers and goes out it may be for any one of a variety of reasons. The wick may have burned out, the oil may be exhausted, the wind may have blown out the flame or the rain extinguished it. But in the eyes of his judges a man's words can only have one meaning, his actions only one motive. There is nothing complex about human nature for a judge; life is quite simple.

Once two friends, drinking together, got into a furious argument and one, in a moment of passion, killed the other. The innkeeper and the customers fled in horror, and the murderer was left alone with his dead friend. Unable to realize what he had done, he only knew that he was parched with thirst, so he went and poured himself out a glass of beer, drained it at a gulp, and, seeing a knife on the floor beside the corpse and realizing it was his, he picked it up and ran out of the inn. At the trial the judge held that his behavior in drinking at such a moment proved not thirst but incredible callousness, and therefore refused to exercise his prerogative of mercy. That glass of beer proved his undoing.

That story passed through my mind as I stood before my judges. They did not seem in the least interested in High Treason. Instead they were bent on discovering whether I had had intimate relations with a certain actress, whether I was sexually diseased. They exchanged significant looks and nodded solemnly to each other. I could think of no logical connection between eroticism and High Treason, and I had no idea whether their findings on my private life would affect the main charge adversely or favorably.

The solemn atmosphere was broken by an amusing interlude. The first witness called was Eisenberger, a farmer Deputy. He was dressed in knee-breeches and gaiters, set off by a green waterproof hat. The judge remarked that his dress was hardly in keeping with the dignity of the Court. "Not good enough, aren't I?" he said. "Then I'll clear out. I've no cause to stay here. And let me tell you that what's good enough for the National Assembly is good enough for this infernal hole!" And anyway the Court had no business to subpoena him, since he was a Deputy, he was, and as such immune. They ought to have asked permission of the Assembly, they ought. However, he couldn't tell them anything; he was only a poor simple farmer, he was. When the judge appealed to his sense of duty and suggested that perhaps he was not quite so simple as all that, he thawed and confided under oath that the accused certainly had seemed to him a pretty poor specimen. "God bless you, sir," he added, and asked where could he get his expenses, for he hadn't got much time; he was a busy man, he was, and must get back to the Assembly at Weimar and draw up Germany's new Constitution.

My Counsel tried to prove that the Government of the moment had itself had an interest in the Soviet Republic and had thus themselves been party to High Treason; but this was too much for the Court to digest. It was simply begging the question. They were far more interested in the state of the books kept by the Red army at Dachau, and whether it

233

was a fact, as some worthy citizen had alleged, that I had left no tip for the house-maid on leaving my headquarters on the battle-field.

Innumerable witnesses were called, some for me, some against me; and I saw how any answer desired may be got out of a witness by clever questioning. I had to defend myself against the imputation of cowardice in not letting myself get killed. I had to try and prove that I was responsible for all my actions, for I knew that they would use the lunatic asylum incident against me if they could, and if they succeeded it was a poor outlook for the Party whose President I was.

I let it be known that such men as Thomas Mann, Björn Björnson, Max Halbe, and Carl Hauptmann had praised my writings, and I was ashamed that this should help mitigate my sentence.

The taking of evidence had already been concluded when the Prosecuting Counsel announced that he would call further witnesses to prove that a military order which I had denied had actually been signed by me. This order had not seriously worried me, although, on the spur of the moment and in a sudden fit of apprehension, I had denied all knowledge of it. But now, I thought, if I am caught in a lie my sentence will probably be increased. I needed all my strength to carry it off, but my courage suddenly deserted me. I faltered and felt uncommonly small. As I was speaking I thought of that other occasion when I had felt so small, when I had denied

234

being the author of our strike leaflet. In a way I wanted the judges not to believe me; however, they did, and the matter was dropped.

Then my Counsel, Hugo Haase, began his speech for the defense. It was the last time he ever defended right against might: four months later, like so many men of the new Germany, he was shot.

"It is absolutely incomprehensible," he said, "that the Revolutionaries of yesterday should charge the Revolutionaries of today with High Treason, and should base their charge on a law designed to protect a Monarchy which they themselves have overthrown. It is absurd for men who themselves achieved power through Revolution to send other men to prison or to death for doing only exactly what they themselves have done. When the Bavarian Diet fled after Eisner's assassination, it automatically renounced its power as a legislative body, yet it still clings to its old prerogatives. The old Ministers have withdrawn from active life, thereby admitting that at the moment the Soviet and not the Diet has the upper hand in Bavaria. Everybody knows that this Soviet Republic was the outcome of a mass movement. When it was established Toller was not even in Munich. On his return he accepted the position as he found it and worked for the new Government. I cannot help calling to mind that Field Marshal Hindenburg, General Groener, von Hintze, the ex-Secretary of State for Foreign Affairs, and innumerable other high officials and army officers also, all solemnly expressed their intention of taking the position as they found it and devoting their services to the Republic. Would my colleague suggest that these men were guilty of High Treason?

"One of the noblest men alive today, a man moreover who protested against war even in the thick of war, Romain Rolland, has interceded most earnestly on Toller's behalf. Toller, I might mention, was recently elected Honorary President of the French Students' Socialist League.

"My colleague has tried to brand Toller as an enemy of his country. Such an allegation seems to me particularly ludicrous at a moment when the Reich Government is everywhere preaching the gospel that now more than ever before every German in Germany has the right to live according to his own lights. My colleague's allegation seems still more remarkable when one reflects that he certainly did not regard the Prussian Toller as an enemy of his country when, with youthful enthusiasm and in the very early days of the war, he joined up with the Bavarian troops. His Bavarian friends, the Bavarian officers who have spoken for him and praised his courage, daring, and sense of duty, have certainly no such opinion of him. Even the Social Democratic newspaper, the *Münchener Post*, has declared that Toller was implicitly trusted by all the workers.

"I am profoundly convinced that it is the duty of this Court to acquit Toller of the charges brought against him."

236

I was asked if I had anything further to say. I had pulled myself together by now, and said:

"Everything I have done I have done soberly and deliberately, and I must ask you to regard me as fully responsible for all my actions.

"I would not be a Revolutionary if I did not allow that force must sometimes be used to change existing conditions. We Revolutionaries recognize the right to revolution only when conditions as a whole have become permanently and utterly intolerable. Then, and only then, do we believe we have the right to overthrow them.

"You will forgive me if I say a word about courts-martial. I can't help wondering what the point of them is. Is it really believed that shooting or imprisoning a few leaders will effectively stem the growing power of the Revolutionary movement among the oppressed workers of the world? Because if so, the strength of this great and fundamental movement is being sadly underrated and the value of our leaders correspondingly overrated!

"Revolution is not an abstract thing; it is made up of the determination of millions of working men; it cannot die until the hearts of all these men have ceased to beat.

"I have heard it said that the Revolution was a purely mercenary movement on the part of the workers.

"Gentlemen, if you would go among the workers for one day you would see for yourselves why these men must satisfy their material needs before doing anything else.

"But they are also struggling with all their energies for the things of the mind; they desire most earnestly to know something of art and culture. The struggle has begun, and not all the persecution of all the united capitalist governments of the world can stop it.

"Gentlemen, I am convinced that the sentence you will pass upon me will be entirely in accordance with the dictates of your conscience and your conception of justice. But I should make it clear that, as I see it, your judgment, whatever it is, will be the judgment of might, not of right."

I was sentenced to five years fortress-imprisonment. I had committed High Treason, but with honorable intent.

15. The Face of the Times

Five or six hundred workmen were defending the railway stations, streets and squares of Munich against an army of a hundred thousand soldiers.

The Stachusplatz was surrounded by two regiments, and for two days my friend Alisi held it with only two machine guns and four men. The machine guns raked the streets that radiated from the place and four men were able to hold in check a whole division.

In the end it was not the enemy that beat them but an old woman. On the third day an officer approached the Stachusplatz to parley. Alisi went to meet him. They met outside a hotel in the Sendlingerstrasse.

"Put your revolver down," shouted the officer.

"Just as you like," agreed Alisi.

"I'll guarantee your safe-conduct if you will evacuate the square."

"Armed or disarmed?" asked Alisi.

"Disarmed!"

"Just to give you a chance of shooting us down! No, thank you!"

239

Then an enormous bosom appeared at one of the hotel windows, and behind the bosom a small, agitated head.

"So you won't come to terms, won't you, you son of a bastard! Who do you think you are, keeping us cooped up here at Your Majesty's pleasure? How long do you think my guests are going to stay here? I never could abide your lazy spit-and-polish ways even when you were the boots here. You that prance about now with your filthy Bolshevism! You do what that soldier says or I'll come down myself!"

In three sentences Frau Sonnenhuber triumphed where an army had failed.

Alisi stared disconsolately at the vision in the window.

"Just as you think best, Frau Sonnenhuber!"

Then to the officer:

"Well, now I hope you're satisfied. You've got what you wanted." And turning back sadly, he and his friends disappeared over the roofs. The last resistance was quelled. The men had fought heroically, but in the end force of numbers told.

The White Terror broke out with bestial ferocity. Seven hundred people were shot—men, women, and children. Thousands were arrested; nobody was safe from informers. The mortuaries proved inadequate and common graves had to be dug as in wartime.

A friend of Graf Arco's, Eisner's assassin, wrote of the shootings in Stadelheim Prison:

"The twelve men who were shot had not the slightest idea that they were being taken to their death; they were led out with hands above their heads and stood in front of the chapel. One of them laughed and said: 'What are they going to do with us now? Prison, perhaps?' Then they were led into the yard, where a number of corpses were sprawled. Too late they realized what was awaiting them, but a volley cut short their cries.

"Next they brought along two women who had seen their husbands casually shot down in the street. As they clung screaming to their husbands' dead bodies one of the soldiers had shouted: 'Let's take the women too!' So they were dragged along to Stadelheim, distraught and disheveled, preceded by a Capucine monk with head bowed in prayer. They died with 'Jesus' on their lips, and were immediately set upon and stripped. All the dead were robbed of their rings and watches."

Schleusinger, a Starnberg law student, wrote:

"There was no doubt that the collapse had begun in earnest. The dull roar of artillery woke me at six this morning, and soon I could make out the rattle of musketry and the tack-tack of machine guns. At eight o'clock I was called to the telephone to hear that General Epp's force was advancing on Starnberg, shooting every Revolutionary at sight.

"At nine o'clock the last meeting of the Workmen's Council began. We passed a resolution that no member of the Workers' Council should leave his post. Just as we were about to disperse, the C.O. of the Red troops arrived with his Adjutant; he could hold out against the Whites no longer, and had been compelled to withdraw. Starnberg was the key to Munich; if Starnberg fell, Munich was completely exposed to the mercy of the Whites as they advanced from the north.

"We calculated that General Epp would take possession of Starnberg at about one o'clock. At one o'clock, then, the Workmen's Council would meet in the Town Hall.

"But the Whites arrived an hour earlier than we expected, and surprised me having lunch. I heard heavy footsteps coming upstairs; no White soldiers appeared, however, only two young members of the *Bürgerwehr* who were helping the Whites.

"As I left the house with my captors a dozen steel-helmeted infantry came marching round the corner, headed by a subaltern in full parade uniform, complete with monocle. 'Are you Schleusinger?' he shot at me. 'Yes, sir,' I answered. 'I'll take you in charge!' and with a wave of his hand he dismissed my original captors. and I was seized by two *Stahlhelm*.

"Soon I was brought before the C.O. of the advance guard. 'Are you the President of the Revolutionary Workmen's Council?' 'Yes, sir.' The Major stamped his foot. 'Take your hand out of your pocket!' I have a crippled arm and generally keep my hand in my pocket. I said: 'You're not my superior officer.' But hardly had I spoken before I was set on from every side, bludgeoned by rifle-butts and hobnailed boots. I sank bleeding to the floor, and should almost certainly have been killed there and then had not an acquaintance of mine, an

242

Austrian army officer, pushed his way through the mob of furious men and protested against such barbaric mishandling. I was taken to prison half-conscious.

"I was by no means the only member of the Red Guard there, and we were all more or less seriously injured. There were workmen there, too, whom I had seen arrested before my own eyes. After the usual formalities I was taken to a cell on the first floor; but I had not been there more than ten minutes when the door opened and a friend, a colleague on the Workmen's Council, was pushed in with me. Blood oozed through the bandages on his head. It was from him I learnt that the Workmen's Council had been arrested *en bloc* and thrown into prison. As they were taken from the Town Hall the crowd jeered and spat and jostled them. Even the military escort had handled them roughly; and one of them had clubbed my friend with his rifle-butt.

"After half an hour I was taken to the Governor's office; an army captain and an N.C.O. sat at the table examining various appeals and decrees which I had signed in the past. They asked if I admitted signing one of the appeals. 'Yes,' I said. 'You're guilty of High Treason.' And, after a moment's pause: 'You are condemned to death. Take him away!'

"Afterwards I discovered that this was called a court-martial.

"It was four o'clock by now, and now began the most ghastly experience of my whole life.

"Above the confused prison noises, the ceaseless shouting and commands, I heard the shuffling tread of the prison Governor coming upstairs, and turned cold. The

243

key grated in the lock. 'This is a bad business, Herr Schleusinger.'

"Two *Stahlhelm* privates rushed in. 'You're to be shot!' A subaltern waited on the landing and lounged downstairs behind me.

"I pulled myself together and followed them out into the street. An officer ran after me. 'What the hell are you doing there? Get back into line!'

"Into line? Then I saw what he meant: more than a score of Red Guards and workmen stood there, most of them wounded and bandaged, guarded by White infantry: the firing party. I've no idea how long we stood there.

"They seemed to be waiting for something, and in due course an official appeared and called over our names, which he entered neatly in a little book; all very proper and methodical, *sine ira et studio*. Then a command, a short drum-roll.

"Terror seized me.

"I marched on automatically, like a clockwork doll; hundreds of eager spectators gaped at us. At last we approached the execution ground.

"Then a dreadful thing happened. In front of us, in the middle of the road, stood a huge gray van; as we approached it swung round to the head of our little column and thereafter preceded us. It gave out a peculiar smell, a sweet carbolic smell like antiseptics and dressings. We would need no more dressings.

"The van seemed to grow and grow till it hung like an ominous shadow over the whole procession; I had a sudden feeling that this vast gray van was the end of all things for me.

"We came to our destination, a field on the outskirts of the town, bounded on one side by a railway embankment. About a hundred yards away a morbidly curious crowd had already gathered.

"We were lined up with our backs to the embankment, and the firing party took up its position about ten yards away. Then one of the condemned men threw himself onto the commanding officer and feverishly, incoherently begged for mercy: he had served on a submarine during the war, but afterwards he could find no work; his father was out of work, too, and his mother was ill; he didn't rightly know what the Reds were doing anyway; it was hunger and poverty that had driven him into the Red Guard. He begged, he implored. It did not help him. He was dragged back against the wall.

"At that moment something unexpected happened; another man, taking advantage of the momentary confusion, sent two of the firing party reeling, knocked down another and made a dash for it. It all happened so quickly that the guard was taken by surprise. They shot, and missed; two men rushed after him, but only succeeded in hindering the fire of the others. The fugitive, lent wings by the fear of death, made for the marshy ground on the far side of the field. Once in the reeds he would be safe. At the last minute luck seemed to fail him; one of the crowd ran across and barred his way with outstretched arms. But the fear of death gave him a giant's strength, and he gave the fellow a blow that sent him reeling. He was safe.

"The firing party turned their attention to us once more.

"The officer pointed to me. 'He's the ringleader;

we'll make him look on, and then he'll know what's coming to him.'

" 'Hands up!' And the poor fellows raised their arms above their heads. 'You are guilty of carrying arms against your Government. Sentence of death will now be carried out.' A thin, half-audible moan came in answer. My heart stood still; I turned half aside to avoid seeing what happened. Carrying arms? I had never in my life carried arms.

"I heard the subaltern's voice giving the order to fire. Then: 'Trying to get out of looking, are you, you swine?' I had to give in; I watched: I saw the poor wretches collapse under the volley; they fell backwards like so many sacks. After the main volley there were a few irregular shots, and one man was still screaming with two bullets in his body. One of the squad went up to within two yards and finished him off.

"The officer turned to me.

"Suddenly a breathless figure appeared running fast toward us. He shouted, gasping for breath. 'Herr Schleusinger . . . it's all right. . . . Wait, Lieutenant, wait. . . . Look, look!' And he waved to the road along which we had come, where another man was running, frantically brandishing a white paper. Arrived, he crushed the paper into the subaltern's hand without a word; the latter glanced at it with a grimace of disappointment.

" 'Take this man back to prison; he's been committed for trial.'

"They took me back to the prison.

"Back again in my cell I collapsed onto the bench. I was saved.

"At ten o'clock that night a friend came to see me and told me that I wasn't the only one who had escaped. One of the men had got two bullets in his lung, which knocked him out without killing him; after several hours he showed signs of life, and the soldiers wanted to finish the poor wretch off; the guardians of order had already stripped him, like the others, of all valuables. But his brother managed to get him taken to the hospital on a stretcher. The soldiers who followed hot on their heels demanded his immediate surrender, but the doctor kept them at bay.

"At eleven o'clock that night my old friend the station master of Starnberg was shot. The prison suddenly echoed with the sounds of moans and cries and supplications that struck us all with horror. Suddenly all was quiet again. A rifle cracked, then another. 'So that's that,' muttered the prison Governor. 'He tried to blow up the railway bridge outside Munich.' I knew better. A fortnight earlier, at an important meeting of the Workmen's Council when Hoffmann's ultimatum fell like a bombshell in our midst, the old fellow had risen to his feet, nervous and bewildered: 'Comrades, I'm an official, a station-master. I have a family to provide for, and I daren't risk my livelihood. I must hand in my resignation from this Council.' We did nothing to deter him. And now he was dead; summarily tried and shot, for all his caution. That man never blew up a bridge.

"At five o'clock on the following evening the prison was filled with the noise of excited talking and shouting and the trampling of feet. Three Red Guards were brought in, streaming with blood. One of them, hardly more than a boy, disfigured beyond recognition, his swollen face all the colors of the rainbow, had twice been put against the wall, twice fallen writhing, twice struggled agonizedly to his feet again."

The Whites never wanted to see our party membership cards. All Republicans were the same to their rifles: Communists, Social Democrats, Independents.

They murdered Eglhofer. A doctor's wife tried to rescue him in her car, but when the car was held up at a crossing he was recognized, arrested, and thrown into a cellar in the *Residenz*. In the cellar a few army officers formed themselves into a Court; he had only to admit that he was really Eglhofer; the admission meant death. They left him in the cellar with only a private to guard him. When the officers had gone the man laid his revolver down on the table and made for the door. But Eglhofer called him back: "Comrade, you have forgotten your revolver. Didn't it occur to you that I might overpower you?"

"We know who you are. We thought . . . But if you don't want to . . ." He shrugged his shoulders and took his revolver back. Some minutes later the death-sentence was carried out.

They murdered Gustav Landauer, in whom the German Revolution lost one of its finest men, one of its greatest spirits. A workman who was with Landauer in his last hours has written thus:

"Amid shouts of 'Landauer! Landauer!' an escort of Bavarian and Württemberger Infantry brought him out

248

into the passage outside the door of the examination room. An officer struck him in the face, the men shouted: 'Dirty Bolshie! Let's finish him off!' and a rain of blows from rifle-butts drove him out into the yard. He said to the soldiers round him: 'I've not betrayed you. You don't know yourselves how terribly you've been betrayed.' Freiherr von Gagern went up to him and beat him with a heavy truncheon until he sank in a heap on the ground. He struggled up again and tried to speak, but one of the men shot him through the head. He was still breathing, and the fellow said: 'That blasted carrion has nine lives; he can't even die like a gentleman.'

"Then a sergeant in the Life Guards shouted out: 'Pull off his coat!' They pulled it off, and laid him on his stomach. 'Stand back there, and we'll finish him off properly!' one of them cried, and shot him in the back. Landauer still moved convulsively, so they trampled on him till he was dead; then stripped the body and threw it into the wash-house."

Ludwig Spörer, whom I met in prison, was both deaf and dumb. On his forehead, between the eyebrows, was a deep red scar. I asked him to write down for me what had happened to him:

"I was in the Red Army, and was taken prisoner on May 2nd. The White Guards led me to a brewery where a subaltern took my personal possessions from me, and then I was handed over to an N.C.O. He took me to the playground of a school and said: 'No need to make a song and dance about it. Just stand with your back to that wall, will you.' I did what he told me without thinking much; I was afraid all right, but everything was happening so quickly that I couldn't grasp it. Then he drew his revolver, took aim, and fired.

"I found myself lying on the ground, my head tilted back; I felt wet, and supposed my head must be in a puddle. But why? I opened my eyes, and saw the sky over me. I tried to recollect what had happened, thinking hard. The man had drawn his revolver, taken aim, fired. That wasn't a dream. But I was not dead. Only wounded, apparently. But where was I wounded? I tried to get up, and then remembered; that would do no good. The N.C.O. was probably still watching from a window, and if he saw I was alive he'd come down and finish me off. So I lay very still.

"How long I lay there I've no idea. After a time I heard someone say: 'Here's one of the Reds!' and I could feel hands groping in my pockets. Then I suppose I must have moved, for one of them said: 'He's still alive!' 'Finish him off then!' said the other. And I felt something cold on my forehead.

"When I came to again it was on an operating table in a large room, with men in white coats round me, and nurses. I saw their lips moving, but I heard nothing. I tried to speak, but I couldn't make a sound. Then suddenly I remembered. 'I'm a dead man!' I made signs to show them that I couldn't speak or hear. Gradually I gathered what had happened.

"The first shot had been diverted by my cigarette-case, and I had merely collapsed with horror and fright. The man who had tried to finish me off had actually put his revolver against my forehead and fired, but because my head was tipped back the bullet had not penetrated the skull. It was only a surface wound, although the scar is so deep you can put your finger in it. Then I was left for dead. When the van came round collecting the dead that evening I was taken to the cemetery with the rest. But I must have moved when they laid me in the earth; and a priest standing by persuaded them to send me to a hospital.

"Now I've had a proper trial and they've given me fifteen months for being a party to High Treason. I shall be transferred to a fortress tomorrow."

So the Bavarian Government had brought this man before the Court after he had twice suffered all the torments of dying, after he had virtually died twice; brought him to Court, solemnly tried him, and solemnly sentenced him to fifteen months' imprisonment.

The Minister of Justice at that time, Müller-Meiningen, was a Liberal. No other single event could throw such a light on the spirit of our justice, the face of our times. The Middle Ages, with its trial by ordeal, kept the prisoner in ignorance of his fate to the end; but after the ordeal he was at least allowed to go free. Yet we who live in the Twentieth Century pride ourselves on our enlightenment and our humanity!

It was not until twenty-one members of the Catholic Working Men's Club had by a blunder been arrested and murdered, brutally shot down by the

Whites in a cellar, that the Government forbade the execution of prisoners without trial.

In the following telegram the War Minister, Noske, thanked the G.O.C. of the White army:

"I am extremely pleased with the discreet and wholly successful way in which you have conducted operations in Munich; please convey my thanks to your troops."

16. Five Years

The engine whistled, and the train drew out of Munich station. Clerks, guards, porters, workmen and girls all crowded round to wave me good-by. *Auf Wiedersehen!"* they cried. Passengers traveling in freedom to the four corners of Europe stared in amazement. "I'll be back in five years," I called. The driver of an engine at the next platform bellowed out: "We'll have you out long before then."

How different it all was from my journey to the military prison in 1918! Then little boys had shouted "Murderer!" after me, and I had felt alone and abandoned, outcast from all things and all men.

But now I was buoyed up by the warmth of comradeship, encouraged and strengthened; I was not alone; I was conscious of hands stretched out to me on every side. Five years was a long time, but I felt strangely carefree; I didn't envy the people in the Pullmans who would wake up early next morning by the Grand Canal of Venice. Even the police inspectors were friendly and kind; they could see which way the political wind was blowing; one never knew. They took great pains to point out that after all they too were only workers doing their job, which they did not relish at all; they had to work like niggers, and it was no easy job to get promotion. And finally, if we ever returned to power, they were sure I would bear them no ill-will. One of them offered me a cigarette, the other a piece of liver sausage. "It's homemade," he explained. "My wife always likes me to take something with me when I travel; you know what women are."

In the next compartment was a girl also on her way to prison, and I asked her how long she was in for. "Six years." "A year more than I." "Pah," she laughed, "I can do that on my head!"

Under the Imperial régime the fortresses had been chiefly used for officers, duelists and insulters of His Majesty and such like. Time did not hang on their hands; they ate and drank and wandered about the town and flirted with all the pretty girls. But this pleasant sort of imprisonment existed no longer; the Bavarian Ministry of Justice had thought out a special brand of punishment for us Socialist prisoners—a mixture of solitary confinement and penal servitude. No walks abroad for us, no cheerful visits from friends and relatives; every letter was censored, and we lived on a dismal boiled diet. Only in one particular did the punishment resemble what had been prescribed by the judge: we were always "Mistered" to show that we were not common criminals. But we never knew whether the rights of today would survive till tomorrow; everything was uncertain; one day the reins would be taut, next day they hung loose. Our treatment was a very fair indication of the alternating strength and weakness of the Government.

At first we were housed in different prisons; but after some months we were all brought together in the old reform school prison at Niederschönenfeld, a dismal, bare three-winged building, sheltering behind high walls in the misty, foggy plain between the Danube and the Lech. The cells were so narrow that leaning against one wall you could touch the opposite wall with your outstretched arm. All day the cell doors were left open and we could walk up and down the narrow corridor. Outside, by the gates, warders watched day and night.

Niederschönenfeld held hundreds of political prisoners, men of every stratum of society, of every conceivable occupation. Most of them hoped that their imprisonment would be for a short time only, that a new revolution would secure our release; the day after tomorrow if not tomorrow; next week if not this week. Whenever they read of a strike in the newspapers they dreamed of a general strike which would be the signal for our release. Anyone who dared cast doubts on their hopes became immediately the object of their implacable hatred. "The only reason why we are still here," one of them said to me, "is because you have no faith."

For the first few months the prisoners lived together like brothers, dividing food and money, sharing emotions and thoughts; they were all seized with a frantic desire for public confession, for publicly revealing the manner of their lives, their deeds and their sins. Everybody had to know everything about everybody else. They admitted their darkest impulses, they passed round letters from their wives and mothers: nothing was concealed, everything revealed. Soon everybody knew everybody else inside out: their manner of life, their way of thinking and speaking; the mechanics of their emotions; their smell, the tone of their voices. They knew precisely how a given question would be answered. At first it was like that; everybody striving to sink his own personality in that of his neighbor's. But soon perpetual propinquity began to gall; past confidences were thrown back in one's teeth; confinement began to oppress, loneliness to embitter.

We turned our backs on the present; only the past bore thinking about. In our talk we resurrected the past; every day, ever hour since the beginning of the Revolution was lived over again and again. Forgotten struggles, outmoded phrases, dead emotions, were all raked up again. While we ate together we argued violently, fanatically; always on one theme—the Soviet Republic; always with one object—world revolution. Those who could not believe that the morrow would dawn with the flame of revolution had a bad time of it; they were traitors, petty-bourgeois, counter-revolutionaries.

The workers' movement in Germany had split up

again and again into insignificant parties, groups, and sects—a process which was repeated among the prisoners. But while ordinary human activity is limited and governed by material considerations, in the rarefied air of prison there was no reality to check extravagant theorizing. Groups were formed which did nothing but persecute and abuse each other; the more they had in common the greater was the hatred between them; one Communist sect would forbid its members to speak to another. It was like the Middle Ages, when monks went to death for the sake of a word or a letter.

A young student with whom I had grown friendly and whose time was just up, slipped into my cell to say good-by in a state of acute embarrassment and uneasiness. Before he left he stammered out, "Please don't tell my friends I came to say good-by to you."

Most intolerable of all were certain doctrinaire intellectuals who idolized the proletariat, made a regular cult of it, and taught the workers to despise all other cults except their own. They imitated ways of living that only direst necessity had thrust upon the working classes. One of the prisoners, an ex-officer of the Imperial army, went about in a coat full of holes which he had made himself.

"Why on earth did you do that?" I asked.

"It is my duty to live like a true member of the proletariat," he answered.

Often when I talked to the working men I could see how thin was the veneer of party doctrine, how

257

close below lay the old instincts, instincts instilled for centuries by the ruling classes, at school, at work, at play.

I remember that when a certain Social Democrat died in 1917 the men at a great Berlin factory sent three representatives to lay a wreath on the grave, and these were advised to wear top-hats and frock-coats. One of them, a nineteen-year-old factory hand, did not possess a top-hat and refused to buy one specially. At last, after interminable discussion, they arrived at the extraordinary and revolutionary conclusion that he need not buy himself a top-hat, but that to uphold the dignity of the working classes he should be lent one.

A farmer who was in the prison, an ardent pacifist, told me how at Christmas in 1919 he read Eisner's Peace Address to a gathering of farmers. He told me how they had really perceived war for what it was, how they had been shaken with horror, and tears had come into their eyes; how he himself could scarcely go on reading.

A few minutes later, talking about the war, we discovered that we had both been on the same front, at Pont à Mousson.

"When were you there?" he asked.

"1915."

"1915? Lord, that was nothing, you just sat tight all day. It was different when I was there, I can tell you. We got a move on then. We got our bayonets properly into the Frenchies' bellies! That was a real picnic, that was!"

Another workman had concocted a private theory to the effect that the root of all evil was the bourgeois woman; stuck-up and wanton, her proper sphere was really the brothel. Once he told me about his own sister:

"She's in service with a very wealthy family; they're frightfully nice. Every Sunday when my sister has her afternoon off the mistress shakes hands with her."

In Munich a man called Adolf Hitler was sentenced to several months' imprisonment for attempting to break up a meeting of the Bavarian Monarchist Party. With a mixed following brandishing sticks and chairs he rushed at the platform and the meeting degenerated into a regular shambles, in which several people were seriously hurt.

This man, Adolf Hitler, managed to collect round him a band of discontented clerks, ex-officers, anti-Semitic students, and dismissed officials. His program was naïve, not to say primitive. The Jews and the Marxists were the enemies within the camp responsible for all Germany's misfortunes. They had stabbed her treacherously in the back while she was still unconquered, and then convinced the masses that Germany had lost the war.

The enemy without was France, a degenerate country, with whom war was unavoidable and therefore necessary. The Nordic German race was superior to all others, and God had called him to weed out from it Jews and Marxists. Hitler goaded his people into a fanatic nationalism. I do not remember hearing Hitler's name when, two years before, we "enemies within the gates" were fighting hard against the injustices of Versailles. During the Revolution, too, he was silent.

One of the prisoners told me that he had met this Austrian house-painter in a Munich barracks during the first months of the Republic. At that time Hitler was calling himself a Social Democrat; my informant had been very unfavorably impressed by the "conceited and puffed-up" way in which he had spoken about his politics, like a man who has read many books and digested none. But he had not taken him seriously because an N.C.O. in the Army Medical Corps told him that when Hitler returned from the front, badly shell-shocked, he was quite blind at first in the hospital, but had suddenly recovered his sight.

That nervous blinding made me thoughtful. A man who can deliberately go blind in face of things he does not want to see, must possess extraordinary strength of mind.

Hitler was being subsidized by a group of wealthy manufacturers, who used him as their cat's-paw while in public he inveighed against the Trades Unions.

Meanwhile the days slipped by, and more and more our speech and thoughts and dreams ran on women.

At night we would bury our heads in the pillows in despair, hungering for warmth. We were tired of the prison books; for hours on end we would pore over the illustrated magazines, gazing at the pictures of naked women, naked breasts, naked legs.

In the Eichstädt prison the women had occupied the floor above ours. The men, excited by such proximity, used to tap on the ceilings of their cells at night, and the girls would answer. They sent notes by the lavatory pipes, rolled up paper tied with string. They started love affairs in which mistress and lover had never seen each other; in clumsy words they tried to describe their appearance to each other. They exchanged keepsakes, locks of hair, little pieces of cloth that had lain against their breasts at night.

In the prison yard there stood a little wash-house where the girls worked during the day, under the supervision of a matron. One day the matron was called away, leaving one girl alone. She gazed out of the window trying to make out the cell of the man with whom she had been corresponding for weeks. She loved him, she wanted to see him; but how should she recognize him? But the man had already seen and recognized her and was waving to her to show that it was he who was her lover. She shook her head incredulously. He pointed to his brown, curly hair, his hooked nose, the scar by his ear. At last she was convinced; she smiled at him and stretched out her arms to touch him just once, to embrace him just once. But the heavy bars of prison stood between them. Then in a moment of overwhelming emotion she jumped back from the window, unbuttoned her coarse gray linen dress and showed him her body, her firm little breasts, her sturdy round legs. She laughed and wept for joy; at last she had been able to do something for him, to show him how much she loved him. Everything she did she did for him alone, and this at last would prove it to him. Neither of them noticed that the matron had returned and was watching. The girl paid dearly for this magnificent gesture of a great and simple heart. She was due to be released the following week, but she lost her remission.

In Niederschönenfeld, however, there were no women, but there were plenty of boys. A young sailor decked himself out with blue ribbons, his hips swaying like a woman's as he walked, and tempted the men; and they let themselves be tempted; he even seduced a warder. Soon other youths were imitating him; there were scenes of violent jealousy; fervent love-letters; a great amount of blushing and hysterical reconciliations. The boys were loaded with presents; many went hungry on their account. At night they slept in one another's cells; no punishment could deter them. The longing to love and be loved broke down all restraints and inhibitions, until finally the tension culminated in a grotesque climax. Some of the prisoners, good orthodox Socialists and respectable citizens, formed themselves into a Court of Love, lasting for days, at which lover and beloved had to defend themselves, and their cases were submitted to the excited arbitration of a judge.

A workman whose wife had been a prostitute, and who had quite easily forgiven her past, came up to me one day.

"Oh, Toller," he said, "what would my family say if they knew I'd been locked up with this sort of gang!"

There was a press war being waged between Bavaria and the Reich. The *Bayerischer Kurier* announced that it had at last discovered the source of the anti-Bavarian propaganda. It all originated in Niederschönenfeld prison. I was the secret agent. I was supposed to be in touch with my cousin Weissmann, the Prussian State Commissary. I was not related to Weissmann, I had never even met him, and, besides that, all my letters were censored. I wrote as much to the Berlin *Freiheit*, but the prison authorities confiscated my letter. I complained to the Bavarian Premier, Graf Lerchenfeld; I had been elected a member of the Bavarian Diet, and even if the Diet prevented me from exercising my high office I at least had the right to communicate telegraphically with the Prime Minister. That telegram also was confiscated. The prison authorities told me through the chief warder that they were not in a position to send telegrams gratuitously. I answered that the authorities had no right to take such a position, but the chief warder cut me short by pushing me out of the room.

"You've no right to lay hands on me!" I cried. "I shall enter a complaint against you."

"I did not touch you, you liar!" shouted the warder.

"You're lying yourself," I retorted.

An hour later I was hauled up before the authorities. I found myself face to face with Public Prosecutor Hoffmann. He was a kind father, I knew, for I had often stood at my barred window and watched him playing with his child. But now he sat there short and square, his blunt chin drawn in, his thick neck held rigid. With one fleshy hand he drummed on the table, with the other he brandished a document at me threateningly:

"It has been reported to me that you called a German a liar."

"I am just as much a German as the warder."

"Answer my question."

"Yes, the chief warder did lie to me; he said . . ."

"You don't deny it then! That's enough. Details can wait. Three days' deprivation of bed, exercise, writing facilities, as well as the usual incidental punishments."

The warder put me into the solitary confinement cell. For some minutes I was unable to realize that any man had such complete power over me. I shouted and beat on the door. The warder opened the door; I seized my stool, and had a sudden horrible realization of how near I was to murder; no one is proof against it.

I felt I must do something to show the Governor that his power was not unlimited. I started a hunger-strike.

The first day you are not troubled by hunger; on the second day, however, you feel a gnawing pain in the stomach; and on the third day you become feverish, and hunger is forgotten in a numbing apathy.

On the evening of the fourth day my special punishments were discontinued. The papers had taken up my case. I broke off my hunger-strike and asked for food. The warder brought me a cup of cocoa made with water and a piece of bread. I gulped them both down ravenously, and found my hunger returning. I waited half an hour until I could bear it no longer, then I asked the warder for another piece of bread.

"The Governor said only one piece."

Another half hour crawled by; I was going mad with hunger.

In Berlin my play *Masse Mensch* was being performed for the first time at the Volksbühne. But all I wanted was one single piece of bread.

I rang for the warder once more.

"What do you want?"

I suddenly shot out at him: "Will you ask the Governor whether I can have some bread!"

He pricked up his ears, like a dog recognizing his

master's voice, and instinctive servility responded to the harshness of my tone; he clicked his heels and went off to the Governor.

A quarter of an hour later my door opened once more. Bread at last!

"I am to tell you that the Governor stands by his decision, and that you are to have no more bread to-night; you have only yourself to blame for hunger-striking. Discipline must be maintained."

The door closed behind the warder, and the light was turned out.

I shall never forget that night. In the darkness I groped about the table for stray breadcrumbs. Next morning I could not even keep the prison coffee down.

The men who had been sent out from Munich to run the prison could never forgive us for not regarding them with awe, for seeing them as the petty creatures they were. They were afraid of us, and their persecutions were in revenge for their own fears.

A London publisher sent me the English translation of *Masse Mensch*. The book was confiscated "for corresponding in a foreign language."

The editor of an anthology asked me to contribute something. I sent him a little story; that was confiscated too. Since I had no other copy I asked for it to be returned to me. "Granted," answered the Governor, "if Toller promises never to reveal that it was once confiscated."

I asked the Governor's permission to keep my hat in a cardboard box. "Permission refused for reasons of safety," ran the answer. "A hat can be kept just as well in a newspaper. Or, since it will not be wanted here, send it home."

I sent a card to a friend in Berlin, bearing the words: "Best wishes from E. T." The card was confiscated for "throwing out veiled hints."

According to regulations we should have been allowed to have daily papers. During a single month the *Frankfurter Zeitung* was confiscated twenty-two times, *Freiheit* twenty times and the *Rote Fahne* thirty times.

M. was punished with solitary confinement because on parade he "made a movement with his left foot indicative of disrespect for the authorities."

W. was given solitary confinement until his "character could be established" because one of the slats in his bed was found loose. W. complained to the Governor, and on the following day was given eight days' plank bed for complaining. He complained of this to the Prison Commissioner, and for daring to complain a second time was put on bread and water for three days. Erich Mühsam ventured to draw the attention of the authorities to the unstable state of W.'s mind. For this Mühsam was punished with seven weeks' solitary confinement. "It will give Mühsam an opportunity to decide whether it is worth while to try and gain leadership by interfering with the affairs of other prisoners," ran the report. Some weeks later W. had to be taken to a hospital.

During a single year the prisoner T. spent one hundred and forty-nine days in solitary confinement, was deprived of writing materials on two hundred and forty-three days, was not allowed to receive parcels on two hundred and seventeen days, was deprived of his bed on fourteen days, of exercise on seventy days, was forbidden visitors on one hundred and sixty-eight days, spent eight days in the dark cell, and on twenty-four days was forbidden any food.

In the Reichstag our treatment was approved by a prominent Bavarian lawyer, who designated the prisoners at Niederschönenfeld as "Red brutes."

Eisner's murderer, Graf Arco, was not among us; he was taken to a special fortress at Landsberg. There was no disciplinary punishment for him: he amused himself as he liked in the town and on the estates round about.

The suffering that man inflicts on man is beyond my comprehension. Are people naturally so cruel? Have they so little imagination that they cannot realize the manifold torments that humanity endures?

I do not believe in the essential "wickedness" of man. I believe that the worst things are done from lack of imagination, from "laziness of heart."

Have I not myself read of famines in China, of Armenian massacres, of the torturing of prisoners in the Balkans, and then thrown the paper aside and proceeded with my usual daily tasks without giving another thought to what I had read? Ten thousand human beings starved to death, a thousand human beings shot—what do these figures mean to me? I read them and in an hour forget them. Lack of imagination. How often have I refused help to those in need? Laziness of heart.

If only the active could realize the true meaning of what they do, and the inactive of what they leave undone, man would no longer be his own worst enemy.

The most important task of the schools of tomorrow is to develop the child's imagination, to conquer this laziness of heart.

Many Socialists mock at the idea of freedom as a bourgeois illusion. They fail to distinguish between freedom as a state of mind, of consciousness, which gives mankind dignity and self-respect; and freedom as a state of being, an outward form. Implicit in every form are its own limitations. Every political and social order must necessarily limit individual freedom; it is the degree of limitation that matters. Laborers and peasants realize this more surely than other men, as they do the necessity for degrees of social rank. Socialism certainly demands equality of opportunity: everybody has the same right to food, shelter and education. But in other ways Socialism

269

must create its own classes. Men who are politically, socially, culturally able will form an aristocracy not of birth but of the mind, an aristocracy of duty, not of material privilege.

The independent newspapers did not flag in their denunciations of the injustices of Niederschönenfeld, and the Bavarian Government retaliated by describing a conspiracy alleged to have been hatched by the prisoners in the fortress. In various newspapers the following appeared under the headline: "Toller and Mühsam attempt new *Putsch*."

"Various significant facts have recently come to light which point to Niederschönenfeld prison as the headquarters of an apparently widely extensive conspiracy, involving High Treason, with the overthrow of the Government and the reëstablishment of the Soviet Republic as its aim. The plot, tested in every detail, was to have been set in motion by the disarming of the *Einwohnerwehr*, and the worst suspicions of the authorities have been confirmed after a thorough search of all the prisoners."

A number of readers must have wondered how on earth a "widely extensive" conspiracy could be initiated by anybody shut up in a prison surrounded by high walls, protected by barbed wire, and bristling with field and machine guns. This inspired paragraph was not intended merely for home consumption; it was also intended to convince France of the necessity of maintaining the *Einwohnerwehr*, whose demobilization she was demanding.

At the time of this "conspiracy" we were forbidden the newspapers; but one morning all the cells were opened, and, clad only in our shirts, we were taken by strange warders to new cells where we were all kept in strict solitary confinement. It was not until some weeks later that we first heard about our conspiracy, and that through a report in a French paper which the Censor had overlooked.

After Rathenau's assassination the Reichstag for the first time called to mind the Republicans pining away in prisons all over the country, and it was decided to grant a general amnesty. How our hopes rose when we heard the news; to be free at last! After three years to be free! We forgot the grayness of our days, the sleepless nights, the inner suffering, the starvation of the mind; forgot the hours of hopelessness and despair; forgot how often we had been nearer death than life. Soon we should be filling our lungs with the air of freedom; soon we should be looking up at the stars on warm summer nights. How far away and half forgotten was the sound of the evening breeze along the grasses. Once more we would be with our friends, with the women whom we loved, the women who loved us. How eagerly we waited for the message which should open the prison doors for us once and for all. We sang and laughed and hugged each other in our joy; all our quarrels were forgotten. We packed up our meager possessions; we put on our best clothes so that when the news came through not a second should be lost in shaking the dust of prison from our feet.

The warder brought me a message. A Reichstag deputy had telegraphed me that the amnesty was confirmed. Dazed with sudden happiness we silently clasped each other's hands.

But what had really happened? For some days we received no newspapers, no letters.

At last we discovered what had happened. The Bavarian Government had proclaimed its independence in the Reichstag, and had declared that the Reich had no authority to release prisoners held in Bavaria. The Reichstag had given in. All other political prisoners were released. Only the Bavarian prisons kept their gates closed.

One prisoner was seized with an epileptic fit when he heard the news; another tried to hang himself. The rest went quietly back to their cells. The walls seemed to suffocate us, so close they were.

One day we discovered that the watch at the prison gates had been strengthened and that all our correspondence with the outer world was temporarily cut off. We lived in a state of excited apprehension, completely in the dark as to what was happening outside. The warders told us when questioned that we were being protected, not punished, and in due course we learned the truth.

Adolf Hitler, whose party had gained ground during the last year or two, had planned a *Putsch* with Ludendorff for November 7th. In a Munich *Bierkeller* Hitler declared the Government overthrown and proclaimed himself Dictator. In the night he had a number of distinguished Jewish citizens arrested, announced a march on Berlin, and swore that on the morrow he would either conquer or die.

In the *Bierkeller* enthusiasm had run high.

Next day when the procession with Hitler and Ludendorff at its head was marching down the Luitpoldstrasse they had found their way blocked by a detachment of *Reichswehr*. Outside the Feldherrnhalle the army opened fire and several National Socialists were killed. Ludendorff and Hitler threw themselves on the ground, a thing for which nobody could blame them, and retreated at the earliest possible moment.

The Minister of Justice had been warned that a group of Nazis was to invade the prison and kill the lot of us; hence the strengthened guard.

Hitler was accused of High Treason, but it was obvious that the Republican judges sympathized with him. He was sentenced to five years in a fortress, a sentence which did not include the term of imprisonment due to him for breaking the peace.

But that's another story.

How differently were my Socialist friends treated. One of them, a youth of eighteen, who was sentenced to fifteen months in a fortress and spent twelve months at Niederschönenfeld, wrote to me after his release to say that he was writing for a Socialist newspaper about the cultural problems of the proletariat. His letter was intercepted, he himself re-arrested and deprived of his good conduct remission.

The assassins of both Erzberger and Rathenau were National Socialists. The papers alleged that they had a secret organization whose task it was to lay dangerous opponents by the heels.

Before Rathenau was killed the Nazi students used to sing:

"The rifles ring out—tack, tack, tack,
On all the swine both red and black
And Mr. Walter Rathenau
Will find his days are precious few:
Let fly at Walter Rathenau
The God-damned dirty Jew!"

I developed a painful abscess, and as there was no dentist at Niederschönenfeld, I was taken by a warder to a near-by town.

It would have been easy enough to escape. We went down a narrow, unfrequented street and came to cross-roads with three other streets. I could have given the warder a shove, run off, boarded the train and got out at the next station. Friends would have helped me and I could have got over the border into Austria. I determined to put the plan into action next time.

Before my next visit to the dentist I had begun to

write my play *Hinkemann*. This time there was another prisoner coming with me; I had told him of my plan, and we had determined to escape together. I made only one condition: he must wait until I had finished my play. Some days later my friend said: "I'm not waiting any longer. Tomorrow I'm going to the dentist; tell them your tooth's hurting you and come too, and we'll get away." I was in the middle of the third act; I intended to write the final scene early the following morning. I had built it up in my mind; I saw every detail vividly; tomorrow I would be able to do it. I knew it. Tomorrow or not at all. I daren't leave it; I daren't interrupt it. I couldn't sleep: should I escape or should I write my play? I chose my play, and my friend went to the dentist without me and escaped quite easily. That day the Minister of Justice forbade further visits to the dentist.

Sometimes I deeply regretted having refused the offer of pardon that was extended to me in 1919 after six months in prison. It was when my play *Die Wandlung* was running. It ran for more than a hundred performances, and the Bavarian Minister of Justice wanted to make a grand gesture and set me free. I refused; to have accepted would have meant supporting the hypocrisy of the Government; besides I stuck at the idea of being freed while others remained behind in prison.

Not every attempt at escape was successful. One of the strangest attempts was made by my friend K.

There was a covered latrine in the yard, and every day he disappeared there for half an hour at a time. He pried up the planks of the floor, dug a hole with his bare hands, dumped the displaced earth into the latrine and replaced the planks. When the hole was deep enough for him to hide in he climbed down and pulled the planks back above his head. We all went back to our cells; he remained bent double in his hole. He intended to crawl out at nightfall, climb the fence and get away. But the warders soon noticed that one of the prisoners was missing. The whole prison was combed fruitlessly. The yard was empty. One of the warders went into the latrine; the planks creaked under his weight; and at that moment my friend coughed. The warder looked round in astonishment. For a moment he half thought that he himself must have coughed. Then my friend coughed again and was discovered.

In the next cell to mine was a fellow called Hans. Often we would sit and talk together and he would tell his experiences. One of these I wrote down.

"I began with three marks fifty pfennigs, and with that I bought a watch from a pawnbroker, which I sold the same day for seven marks. With this money I bought two watches and made a corresponding profit. At times I used to meet other hawkers, and from them I picked up a new trick. One of them dealt in Holy Pictures and bottles with pieces of wood floating in spirits. He told me he sold them at a high price to the peasants as Holy Relics, calling the wood bits of the Holy Cross. Obviously that could only be done in lonely districts where there was no railway and where the people were still completely under the thumb of the priests. I wrote at once to Munich for a supply of Holy Pictures, bought some little glass tubes and got them up to look like the reliquaries I had seen. I got forty marks for one, and I didn't sell any for less than ten marks. The pictures, which cost a few pfennigs, I sold for fifty pfennigs. But I managed to beg so much meat, butter, and eggs into the bargain that I had plenty over every day to sell to the innkeepers. The peasants looked on me as a saint. To make myself look the part I got a fellow to make me an Italian cloak, and told everyone that I came from Rome.

"When I had cleaned up the Bavarian woods I went off to Tyrol with my pictures and watches. I had rings as well, for all sorts of people—rings for whores, for instance, all symbolic, or carved with an owl for keepers.

"One day I was talking with a peasant, and he made such a fuss over me, that I grew bolder and thought— If you're so stupid about the pictures and the relics I'll give you something to think about, I will! I told him I'd been to Rome, and a lot more on the same lines. He was fairly amazed at all the places I'd been to. 'That's right,' I said. 'The true pilgrim has to sell all he has and wander eternally through life; and the great drawback is that he can never satisfy the greatest vital need of man; he can never know the love of woman. It never happens in Austria,' I went on, 'as it has happened to me in Italy. There I've met peasants who have really understood, who've said to me—you can even take my wife

277

if you like.' 'No,' said the peasant, 'we don't do that sort of thing here.' 'That's just it,' I said. 'In Italy they really honor the pilgrims, while here—' And he said, 'Yes, it would be all right if my old woman were not so sensitive about that sort of thing; but she wouldn't hear of it.' He was sure. 'I'll talk to her, and you'll see for yourself.' That evening I slept in the same bed with them both. His wife was in the middle, with him on one side and me on the other. And sure enough he went off to sleep. 'Aren't you pleased having a holy pilgrim like this?' I said. And it's a fact she was."

The more I became used to prison life, the more it became a mere matter of routine, the more time I had for thinking, and was increasingly oppressed by my recollections of the Revolution.

I felt at odds with myself. I had always believed that Socialists, despising force, should never employ it for their own ends. And now I myself had used force and appealed to force; I who hated bloodshed had caused blood to be shed. I remembered how in Stadelheim an opportunity for escape had presented itself and I had refused to take advantage of it lest my flight should cost a warder his life. A great deal had happened since then. I meditated on the position of men who try to mold the destiny of this world, who enter politics and try to realize their ideals in face of the masses. Was Max Weber right after all when he said that the only logical way of life for those who were determined never to overcome evil by force was the way of St. Francis? Must the man of action always be dogged by guilt? Always? The masses, it seemed, were impelled by hunger and want rather than by ideals. Would they still be able to conquer if they renounced force for the sake of an ideal? Can a man not be an individual and a mass-man at one and the same time? Is not the struggle between the individual and the mass decided in a man's own mind as well as fought out in the community? As an individual a man will strive for his own ideals, even at the expense of the rest of the world. As a mass-man social impulses sweep him toward his goal even though his ideals have to be abandoned. The problem seemed to me insoluble. I had come up against it in my own life, and I sought in vain to solve it.

It was this conflict that inspired my play *Masse Mensch*. I was so oppressed by the problem, it so harassed and bewildered me, that I had to get it out of my system, to clarify the conflict by the dramatic presentation of all the issues involved.

I wrote the play in a very few days. The lights were turned out every evening at nine o'clock, and we were not allowed candles; so I lay on the floor under the table and hung a cloth over it to conceal the light of my candle. All night until morning I wrote in that way.

It had a remarkable reception when it was first put on by the Municipal Theatre at Nürnberg. Some people held that it was counter-revolutionary in so far as it was an indictment of force; others insisted that it was pure Bolshevism because the apostles of non-resistance went under in the end.

Some critics also accused the play of tendentiousness; but what would not have been tendentious in their eyes? Only a play which implied wholehearted acceptance of the existing order.

There is only one form of tendentiousness which the artist must avoid, and that is to make the issue simply between good and evil, black and white.

The artist's business is not to prove theses but to throw light upon human conduct. Many great works of art have also a political significance; but these must never be confused with mere political propaganda in the guise of art. Such propaganda is designed exclusively to serve an immediate end, and is at the same time something more and something less than art. Something more because, at its best, it may possibly stimulate the public to immediate action; something less because it can never achieve the profundity of art, can never awaken in us the tragic sense of life, or, as Hebbel puts it, "rouse the world from its sleep."

Art in its greatest, purest manifestations is always timeless; but the poet who wishes to reach the heights and penetrate the depths must take care to specify particular heights and particular depths, or he will never catch the public ear, and will remain incomprehensible to his own generation.

As for *Masse Mensch*, all further performances were banned by the Bavarian Government, even those already contracted for. The Government's action was based on a complaint from the German-Jewish Citizen's Union which took umbrage at the scene in the Stock Exchange.

Living in intimate touch with so many people enriched my knowledge. I learned more of the working classes there than a thousand books and statistics could have taught me. I read their letters from home and the answers they wrote back; I came to know intimately their needs and their joys, their weaknesses and their virtues; I realized how much splendid strength was caged up in Niederschönenfeld. Prison gave many of them their first chance to read; and how eagerly they seized upon it! One of them who scarcely knew the meaning of the word philosophy began to study Kant; his head whirled with the first half dozen lines; but soon he found he could grasp the most abstruse philosophical problems. Others, disillusioned, withdrew from politics and devoted themselves to theology. Communism for them transcended politics and became a sort of metaphysical nostalgia. They merely smiled when their more matter-of-fact friends called them renegades. I found I had to abandon the stereotyped picture I had formed in my own mind of the "proletariat." I began to see the workers as they really were.

The conscious, active proletarian of the twentieth century, the product of machines and great cities, is neither a saint nor a god; he is the historical standard-bearer of an idea, of Socialism. He is part and parcel of the contemporary system of government and class-distinctions: when Socialism fulfills itself and abolishes arbitrary class-distinctions the proletariat will be no more. Are the "enlightened" masses of the twentieth century any more reliable than the "unenlightened" masses of the ninteenth? How easily the masses are still swayed by whims, by promises and hopes of self-advantage; how easily they still drop one leader for another. Today they cheer a man, tomorrow they damn him. At one moment they will stand by their principles; an hour later abandon them. How easy it is for gifted orators to rouse them to passionate action. In Niederschönenfeld I came to know the social conditions which underlie this spiritual instability, the great evil of today which cripples strength of purpose—the dependence of mankind on the labor market, on machines. I used to think that the power of reason was so strong that he who had once seen reason could not but follow it. But experience is soon forgotten; the path of the people is laborious; the people themselves, not their opponents, are their own greatest enemy.

This conflict and the instability of rebels and revolutionaries, the struggle of man against machinery, I tried to picture in my play *Die Maschinenstürmer*. I found many parallels of our own struggle in the history of the Luddites.

On the day of its first performance in Max Reinhardt's *Grossem Schauspielhaus* in Berlin, Rathenau

282

was assassinated by student members of the People's Party. In the last act when the people, goaded by a traitor, rise up and kill their leader, the whole house of five thousand people rose up as one man. The stage had become the mouthpiece of the people.

On the wall of my cell the sun threw two oval patches of light, and staring at them I suddenly wondered how the world would seem to a man who had been emasculated in the war. Surely health must blind us to so much. A few minutes later I wrote down the argument of my play *Hinkemann*.

Even Socialism can only heal the suffering which arises directly from the inadequacies of the social system; there will always be suffering. But such man-made suffering is senseless and unnecessary; man-made suffering at least is curable.

When *Hinkemann* was performed at the Dresden State Theatre there was a riot. It was instigated by a National Socialist manufacturer who appropriated the funds of a welfare club and bought eight hundred tickets, which he distributed among students, clerks, and schoolboys. Each of the eight hundred was given a paper with the anti-war sentences from my play on it, which were to be signals for general uproar. The first scene came to an end and the eight hundred stared at each other in dismay; their cue was missing; the producer had cut it. But in the second scene their chance came and there was no holding

283

them; they yelled and whistled and bawled the national anthem.

One episode in the play was translated into real life. In one of the boxes a man collapsed with heart-failure in the midst of the uproar; those who were near-by begged the rowdies to have some consideration for the dying man. One of them bent over the man, coolly studied him, saw the arched nose, and turning to his companions said: "It's only a Jew!" They went on shouting.

I thought of my own childhood, of my misery when the other children shouted "Dirty Jew!" at me, of my childish appeal to the picture of Christ; of my terrible joy when I realized that nobody would recognize me for a Jew; of the first day of the war and my passionate longing to prove that I was a real German by offering my life to my country; of my writing from the Front to the authorities to say that they could strike my name from the list of the Jewish community. Had it all been for nothing? Had it all been wrong? Did I not love Germany with all my heart? Had I not stood in the rich beauty of the Mediterranean landscape and longed for the austere pine-woods, for the beauty of the still, secret lakes of North Germany? And was not the German language my language, the language in which I felt and thought and spoke, a part of my very being?

But was I not also a Jew? A member of that great race that for centuries had been persecuted,

284

harried, martyrized and slain; whose prophets had
called the world to righteousness, had exalted the
wretched and the oppressed, then and for all time, a
race who had never bowed their heads to their perse-
cutors, who had preferred death and dishonor. I had
denied my own mother, and I was ashamed. It is an
indictment of society at large that a child should have
thus been driven to deception.

But was I an alien because of all this? Is blood
to be the only test? Does nothing else count at all?
I was born and brought up in Germany; I had
breathed the air of Germany and its spirit had molded
mine; as a German writer I had helped to preserve
the purity of the German language. How much of
me was German, how much Jewish? I could not
have said.

All over Europe an infatuated nationalism and
ridiculous pride was raging—must I too participate in
the madness of this epoch? Wasn't it just this madness that had made me turn Socialist?—my belief that
Socialism would eliminate not only class hatreds but
also national hatreds?

The words, "I am proud to be a German" or "I
am proud to be a Jew," sounded ineffably stupid to
me. As well say, "I am proud to have brown eyes."

Must I then join the ranks of the bigoted and
glorify my Jewish blood now, not my German?
Pride and love are not the same thing, and if I were
asked where I belonged I should answer that a Jewish
mother had borne me, that Germany had nourished

285

me, Europe had formed me, my home was the earth, and the world my fatherland.

One day our friend Hagemeister died. He had been ill for a week, and feeling death near him he asked to be removed to the hospital; but the Ministry of Justice refused permission. They took him away from us, and, as this "humane" prison could boast no sick-room, he was laid in one of the "solitary" cells, and was given a shell case on which to knock if he wanted anything. The prison doctor said he was malingering.

Two days before his death his wife came to see him, but the dying man was not allowed to see her alone. Back in Munich she fought for his life, hurrying in her desperation from one authority to another; but her entreaties fell upon deaf ears.

He died in the night, utterly alone. "Died peacefully in his sleep," wrote the prison Governor.

We were allowed to see our dead friend before they took him away. He was sitting in the bare cell, his head sunk on his breast, one hand lying clenched beside the empty shell case on the folding table, the other hanging limply at his side. The warders were upset and the Governor feared a mutiny. He found our quietness uncanny, and had a machine gun posted on the roof of the building to cover the yard.

We went out into the yard, and nobody spoke a word; silently we demonstrated against the murder, without flags or speeches or any word at all. Round and round we marched in single file; silent; dumb. Round and round for an hour. The guard outside the prison was strengthened, the warders raised the alarm, soldiers crouched by the machine gun. We paid no attention to them. Round and round the yard we went in single file, one behind the other. Silent. Dumb.

In the spring a pair of swallows nested in my cell; they lived with me all the summer. The nest was built, and the female brooded on her eggs while the male sang his little twittering song to her. The eggs were hatched and the parents fed their young and taught them to fly, until one day they flew away and did not come back. The parents had a second brood, but a premature frost killed the young, and they huddled close together silently mourning their dead children. With the coming of autumn they flew away to the southern sun.

That summer was very kind to me. The shy little birds became so used to me that they would come and sit on the lamp when I was working at my table and twitter playfully together. I was very quiet in my happiness and thankfulness.

All that I saw and heard and felt and thought, I wrote down in a little book which I called *The Swallow Book*. Nothing could have been more innocuous, but the Governor confiscated the manuscript. The bald official explanation for this was that the poems were simply cover for subversive propaganda.

I sent a letter of complaint to the Reichstag:

"I have never asked for special consideration, and even now it is not consideration I am asking for but merely the confirmation of my rights as a special political prisoner. Even under the barbaric tyranny of the knout in Tsarist Russia it was possible for imprisoned writers to keep the freedom of their minds. In the Bavarian Free State in this year of grace, 1923, freedom of the spirit is punished as a crime.

"I said nothing when the fortress authorities forbade me a few months ago, in direct contravention of the law, to discuss my health with a visiting relative who was also a doctor.

"I have scorned to complain in the past about various other incidents which were in direct contravention of the terms of my sentence.

"I have scorned to complain when the Bavarian authorities in the Diet and through the press have thrown mud at me in my completely defenseless state.

"I have scorned to complain when the fortress authorities have prevented me from getting an exact idea of the nature of these attacks by confiscating newspapers.

"I have refrained from signing the innumerable petitions presented by the prisoners here to various authorities outside.

"One thing certainly I could not be silent about: that was when I accused the prison doctor of criminal neglect after the shocking death of August Hagemeister. On that occasion I learned that Socialist prisoners in Bavaria have not even the rights of common criminals: I was never allowed to give evidence.

"But now I appeal to the German Reichstag.

288

"Are you prepared to tolerate the suppression of works of German literature by prison officials whenever the spirit so moves them? Are you prepared to tolerate the virtual outlawing from the German Republic of a prisoner just because he is a Socialist?"

The Reichstag did not favor me with a reply, so I had to help myself. A friend wrote down *The Swallow Book* in minute writing on a single sheet of paper, and a prisoner who was being released managed to smuggle it out of prison with him and sent it to be published.

The Governor revenged himself in his own inimitable way. Birds will never build in a covered space except when the window opens to the east, therefore I was transferred to a cell facing north.

In the spring the swallows returned from who knows what primitive forests and blazing sunshine. They picked out our prison from a hundred other prisons and my old cell from a hundred other cells and began to build their nest. Then, at the Governor's command, warders clattered into the cell and callously tore down the almost completed nest.

I thought of the bewildered misery of the swallows when they found their little house gone, how they must eagerly have explored with their little beaks the wall where their nest had been, fluttering anxiously round, searching in every corner of the cell. But next day they had already begun to build again, and again the warders destroyed their work.

The new occupant of my cell, a builder from a Bavarian village, wrote to the Governor.

"Honored Sir,

"I beg you leave the swallows in my cell to nest in peace, they have worked so patiently and been sore tried, also they are industrious and useful. I should like to say that the above do not disturb me in the least, nor do they dirty the cell. Also that I have known other prisons where swallows nest and anybody who disturbs them is punished.

"Yours faithfully,

"Rupert Enzinger of Kolbermoor."

The Governor in answer merely observed that stables were the proper place for swallows to build in, and they would find plenty of room elsewhere.

The nest which the birds had in the meantime been building again was accordingly destroyed, and the prisoner, like myself, transferred to a cell facing north. The swallow cell was locked.

Then the swallows, bewildered and passionately eager, began to build three nests simultaneously in three different cells. But they were only half finished when the warders discovered them and repeated the outrage.

With the energy of despair they started six nests simultaneously. Perhaps they hoped that one nest might be spared them as a gesture of generosity.

But the six nests were all torn down.

I don't know how many times the process of building and destruction was repeated. The struggle lasted for seven weeks; a glorious and heroic struggle between the united forces of Bavarian law and order

290

and two tiny birds. After the nests were torn down for the last time some days went by without a new nest being discovered; evidently the swallows had given up.

But soon whispers were going round among the prisoners that the swallows had found a new place in the wash-house behind the overflow pipes where nobody would find them—neither the spying warders without, nor the spying warders within. Rarely had we experienced a purer happiness. The swallows had won after all in their fight against human beastliness. Their victory was ours too.

But even this nest was doomed to discovery.

After that the swallows built no more. In the evening they would fly into a cell and spend the night huddled close together. In the morning they would fly away. One evening the male swallow came alone; the female was dead.

It was the last year of my sentence. Until now my will to freedom had been unconquerable, unbroken by punishment or illness; but now that I could count the days to my release, something strange happened to me: my eagerness for life ebbed away. I lay all day apathetic in my cell; I did not rejoice in my impending freedom. I dreaded it.

I dreaded the duties and responsibilities which would call me. In the prison I was protected from reality; prison was like a mother to me, a cruel mother who yet ordered my days, fed me, released me from all outer cares. And now I would have to leave the sheltering walls and go out into the world where new struggles awaited me. Would I be equal to it? I had received thousands of letters during my imprisonment; so many people were looking to me, imagining me greater than I really was; they expected great things of me and I should only disappoint them. I felt myself weakening from day to day. The nights were darkened by thoughts of death; my pulse grew fainter, and I longed for death, and when death did not come I was lost in a confusion of horrible temptations. There was a night when I almost took my life. But in the morning my foolishness had vanished. My strength increased; I could only be what I was. I wanted to stand up to life; and stand up to it I would. If defeat came I would learn to endure it.

The day before my release I was called before the Governor, who smiled at me in quite a friendly way.

"I have two messages for you, Herr Toller," he said, "one pleasant, the other not so pleasant. Let us get the unpleasant one over first. You are a Prussian, and the authorities are convinced that you have not changed your outlook during the last five years, which means that you are just as dangerous to the safety of the country as ever you were before, and we can only render you innocuous by keeping you away. So to make sure that you leave Bavaria you will be personally conducted over the border. You yourself will be called upon to meet the cost of your transportation. And now for the pleasant message.

You were to be released at eighteen minutes past one tomorrow, but we are letting you go a day earlier. You can return to your friends today. These two gentlemen"—he indicated the two detective sergeants who bowed and touched their caps—"will accompany you across the borders of Saxony."

"What time is the next train?" I asked.

"You needn't worry about that, Herr Toller. We ourselves have chosen the route especially to avoid big towns and industrial centers where the workers might conceivably want to demonstrate. Obviously all you want now is peace and quiet; and in spite of going by a somewhat roundabout way you will reach the border safe and sound on the morning of July 16th. In short, we make you a present of several unexpected hours of freedom."

I was not allowed to go back to my friends. I had to strip and submit to body and clothing being thoroughly searched. I packed up my things, and, with a detective sergeant on either side of me, walked out through the prison gates. I was free. I breathed in the air of the unbarred sky. The road to the station was patrolled by a cyclist detachment of the *Landjäger* who rode like trick cyclists, curved and graceful, and at the station itself was a special company of heavily armed police.

"What have I done to deserve such honor?" I asked.

"There was to be an attempt on your life," one

of the detectives answered. "And as the Bavarian Republic is responsible for you until you're over the border, it's doing the handsome thing by you so that you'll always have friendly memories of us."

At the border they left me in the train.

I was alone.

I was free.

I stood at the carriage window and looked out into a night of friendly stars.

I thought of some lines in my *Swallow Book:*

"Through the barred window I gaze into the night
The swallows twitter in their dreams
I am not alone.
The moon and the stars are my companions too
And the gleaming, silent fields."

No, I had never been alone all those five years, never alone in my comfortless abandonment. The sun and the moon had consoled me, the wind that flurried the puddles in the yard, the grass that sprang up in spring in the cracks of the stones.

All these were my friends, telling of greetings from the world outside, of comradeship among the prisoners, of belief in a world of justice, of freedom, of humanity, in a world without fear and without hunger.

I was thirty.

My hair had turned gray.

I was not tired.

Lightning Source UK Ltd.
Milton Keynes UK
UKOW050553060612

193899UK00001B/90/P